Still-life photography by Steve Moss

1639
This edition published in 1992 by Tiger Books International PLC, London
© 1985 Coombe Books
Printed and bound in Singapore
All rights reserved
ISBN 1-85501-216-2

The publishers wish to thank the following for
the loan of colour transparencies
relating to French, Spanish and New Zealand wines:

Food and Wine from France, 41 Piccadilly, London SW1
Vinos de España, 23 Manchester Square, London W1
Dent & Reuss Ltd, Plough Lane, Hereford

Enjoying Wine

Alice King

TIGER BOOKS INTERNATIONAL
LONDON

CONTENTS

Introduction

Although wine is today produced around the globe, it was in Europe that the distinctive varieties were developed. Below: three South Sea Islanders enjoy a bottle of New Zealand wine, and (inset bottom right) Cabernet Sauvignon grapes growing in California's Napa Valley. Right: the vineyards of Champagne, which have given their name to the dry, sparkling wine of the area, and (inset bottom left) a taster in Armagnac samples the spirit for which the region is so famous.

Wine is made to be enjoyed, and drinking it should be fun!

It doesn't matter if you know nothing at all about wine. The most important thing is to drink what you like – after all, why should you spend your cash on a wine you don't enjoy just because some 'expert' says it's good? The best way to find out about wines is by experimenting with different ones and, once you find one you like, to remember its name. Having got to this stage you can make life more interesting by trying other wines made from similar grapes or from the same region.

This book is a basic guide to the most widely available wines, their tastes and styles. It is not in any sense the last word as there are literally hundreds of wine books which go into far greater depth on specific wines and regions. I have tried to set the scene and highlight the value-for-money wines on the market. Just because a wine is expensive does not necessarily mean it will be the best value.

Don't be put off by people who sound as if they know a lot about wine. Your choice is just as valid as theirs, and they will buy what they like – why shouldn't you! In any case, a large number of people who talk a lot about wine don't necessarily know much about it.

Hopefully, by reading this book you'll have some idea about where to start, but the great thing about learning about wine is that you have to keep experimenting.

What exactly is Wine?

Right: the Chardonnay grape, which is grown widely throughout the world, but which perhaps finds its finest expression in the strong, dry wine of Chablis Grand Cru (facing page), grown only in seven small vineyards around the French town of Chablis. Below: the firm Cabernet-Franc grape, often used in the production of rosé wines.

Apart from being a drink, wine is the naturally fermented juice of grapes.

After the grapes have been picked and crushed, the skins are taken away from the juice if making a white wine. You may be surprised to learn that most red grapes have white juice. So how is red wine made? The colour comes from the skins which are left in contact with the juice for varying lengths of time depending on whether a red or a rosé wine is being made. The skins add colour and tannin, a bitter substance also found in tea, which gives the wine body and helps it to age.

The wine ferments because of the natural sugars in the grapes. In a dry wine the natural sugar is totally fermented out, whereas in a sweet white wine some of the natural sugar is left in the wine.

Over the past 50 years wine-making technology has improved greatly and the vast majority of wines now available are well-made, if not always to everyone's taste.

The choice of wines on sale in Britain is enormous and increasing all the time, with wines from as far flung places as California and China.

How Wine is Made

The French vine is one of the most cared-for fruit plants: (below) productive European buds grafted onto parasite-resistant American root-stock; (right) the traditional French method of ploughing in March; (bottom left) pruning in January; (bottom right) a careful inspection of the vines in early spring and (facing page) dusting the vines in winter against disease.

Due to its very nature, the grape harvest has to be gathered by hand (these pages) and the people of France have become expert at

collecting and grading grapes. Facing page: the vineyards around the German castle of Burg Stamleck.

The pressing of the grapes (these pages) in October is one of the most important operations in wine production, affecting so much the quality of the final result.

In Champagne (right and facing page right) the grapes are pressed and the juice extracted at once. In Beaujolais (bottom right) the skins of the red grapes are left with the juice to impart their all-important colour and tannin to the wine.

Cellarcraft (these pages), with all its attendant skills, is vitally important for the production of wines which require ageing.

Styles of Wine

Facing page: two similar bottles of Spanish wine, though the paler, dry variety contains 0.6 percent sugar and the sweet wine ten times as much.

Choosing a wine from the huge selection on offer can be a difficult task. However, some shops and supermarkets have now introduced a coding system which indicates the sweetness of the wine. The best of these is a rating of 1 to 9, when 1 is a very dry wine like Muscadet and 9 is a very sweet wine like Sauternes. A medium sweet wine like Liebfraumilch would be rated around 5. By this method, if you know what a particular wine tastes like but if you want something a little drier or sweeter, you simply select one up or down the scale.

This system is generally only used for white and rosé wines because reds, apart from Lambrusco, are normally dry. Reds are often coded according to their style e.g. light-, medium- or heavy-bodied.

Many wines have informative back labels which indicate the style of the wine, where it is produced, how to serve it, and what are the best foods to eat with it.

The following table is a general guide to some of the most widely available wines, divided into their different styles.

WHITE: dry; light- to medium-bodied
Alsace
Bordeaux (dry, e.g. Entre-deux-Mers)
Fino Sherry
Frascati
Luxembourg wines
Mâcon
Muscadet
New Zealand Müller Thurgau
Rioja (new style)
Sancerre
Sauvignon de Touraine
Sercial Madeira
Soave
Spanish (new style)
Sparkling wines (most brut ones)
Swiss wines
Trocken (Germany)
Vin de Pays
Vinho Verde

WHITE: dry; full-bodied
Chablis
Côte d'Or white Burgundies, e.g. Meursault, Chassagne,
Graves
Rhône, e.g. Châteauneuf-du-Pape
Rioja (old-style)

New World Chardonnay/Sauvignon (most)
Vouvray (can be semi-dry)

WHITE: medium sweet; light- to medium-bodied
Amontillado Sherry
Asti
Bual Madeira
German wines up to Kabinett quality
Laski Riesling
Liebfraumilch
Orvieto
Vouvray (demi-sec)

WHITE: sweet; full-bodied
Beerenauslese
Cream Sherry
Côteaux du Layon
Late-picked wines
Liqueur Muscats (Australian)
Malmsey Madeira
Moscatel de Setubal
Muscat de Beaumes de Venise
Sauternes/Barsac
Spätlese
Tokay Aszu
Trockenbeerenauslese
Vouvray Moelleux

RED: light-bodied
Alsace
Beaujolais
Bourgueil
Chinon
Claret (Generic)

German
New Zealand
Sancerre
Saumur Champigny
Valpolicella
Vin de Pays

RED: medium-bodied
Barbera
Chianti
Clarets (good vintage ones)
Côte d'Or Burgundy
Côte-du-Rhône
Dão
Navarra
Rioja
St. Emilion/Pomerol
Zinfandel (or full-bodied)

RED: heavy- to full-bodied
Barbaresco
Barolo
Bull's Blood
California Cabernet/Shiraz
Clarets (Good vintage ones)
Rhône (Better quality ones, e.g. Côte Rôtie, Hermitage, Châteauneuf-du-Pape)
Rioja
Roussillion

RED: sweet
Lambrusco (light)
Port (heavy)
Zinfandel (late-picked)

BottleShapes

Many areas of Europe produce their wines in distinctive shapes of bottle, based upon traditional designs. Far left: the claret bottle, which is ideal for stacking and laying down and is used by many bottlers throughout the world. Left: the Burgundy, which is used for both the red and white wines of the region. Below: the bocksbeutel, based on an old drinking flagon, is popular in Franconia and Portugal. Right: the Alsace flute, a slightly elongated version of the German flute.

Reading the Label

In France the Chateau, where the vines are grown and the wine produced, is of vital importance. Above: the Chateau of Clos de Vouguet, which produces some of the finest wine on the magnificent Côte de Nuits.

The vast majority of wine made, sold and drunk throughout the world is table wine. The label will state the country of origin, but not the region of origin, and the wine can indeed be from several regions. In France the next stage up is Vin de Pays – literally 'country wine' – which states the area of origin. Then there is VDQS – Vin Delimité de Qualité Supérieur, VDQS wines will state on the label which region of France they are from.

Appellation Controlée (or AC) is the top quality designation in France, and refers to specific regions like Appellation Beaujolais Villages Controlée or Appellation Bordeaux Controlée. Many areas have several small ACs within them. For instance, in Bordeaux you also find AC Pauillac, AC Médoc, etc. In general, the more specific (or smaller) the Appellation is, the better the wine is likely to be. For example, AC Margaux will be better than AC Bordeaux.

In Italy the equivalent is DOC (Denominazione di Origine Controllata), and a few of the top quality regions have

MIS EN BOUTEILLES AU CHATEAU —————— Bottled at the chateau

CHÂTEAU MÉAUME

1982

BORDEAUX SUPÉRIEUR

PRODUCE OF FRANCE

APPELLATION BORDEAUX SUPÉRIEUR CONTROLÉE.

750ml

GIP·LIBOURNE

K.A. JOHNSON-HILL PROPRIÉTAIRE A MARANSIN (GIRONDE)

Name of chateau

Quality status which will give the name of the region

Vintage

Country of origin

Contents

Name of chateau owner

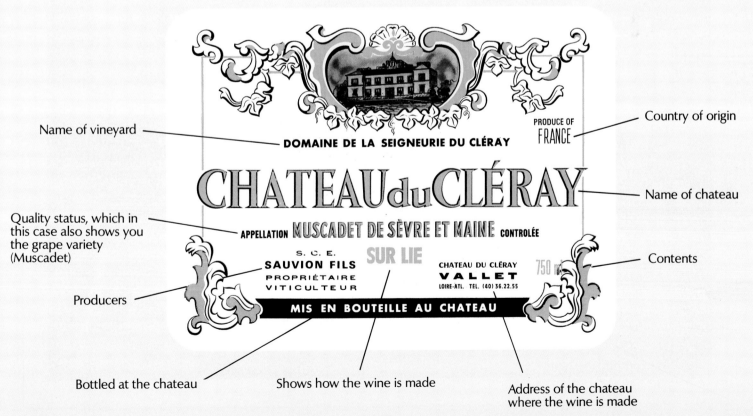

DOMAINE DE LA SEIGNEURIE DU CLÉRAY

PRODUCE OF FRANCE

CHATEAU du CLÉRAY

APPELLATION MUSCADET DE SÈVRE ET MAINE CONTROLÉE

S. C. E.
SAUVION FILS
PROPRIÉTAIRE
VITICULTEUR

SUR LIE

CHATEAU DU CLÉRAY
VALLET
LOIRE-ATL. TEL. (40) 36.22.55

750 m

MIS EN BOUTEILLE AU CHATEAU

Name of vineyard

Country of origin

Name of chateau

Quality status, which in this case also shows you the grape variety (Muscadet)

Contents

Producers

Bottled at the chateau

Shows how the wine is made

Address of the chateau where the wine is made

now been granted a higher designation, DOCG, where the G stands for Garrantia (guaranteed).

Germanic-looking bottles are often, in fact, EEC wine – a Euroblend which, although Germanic in style, can come from any one or more EEC country.

Tafelwein (table wine) is Germany's basic wine quality, and above that comes Landwein – equivalent to Vin de Pays and coming from specific regions. However, the majority of German wine found in Britain is QbA (Qualitätswein bestimmte Anbaugebiete). Above this is the top classification, QmP (Qualitätswein mit Prädikat), with Prädikat refering to the sweetness levels. QmP wines are then classified according to the maturity of the grapes in ascending sweetness levels from Kabinett through Spätlese, Auslese, Beeranauslese to Trockenbeerenauslese which is the sweetest.

In Germany the area in which a wine is grown is important and village names often appear on the label. Right: the village of Punderich and surrounding vineyards. Below: an array of wines, on the pavement at Périgueux, France.

ITALY

Type of wine

Quality status

Brand name

Where bottled

Bottler

Contents

Country of origin

GERMANY

Producer & bottler

English importers

German for sub-district within the eleven regions

The grape variety (eg Müller-Thurgau) can also be shown here

Official testing number

Brand name

The specified growing region – one of eleven in Germany

Name of the village the grapes come from

Quality status. If QmP the sweetness level (eg Spaetlese) will be shown

Contents

Vintage Guide

The year in which a wine is produced, known as the vintage, can be of crucial importance, being recorded on the label (below). In Champagne most wine is blended, but some out-standing vintages may be kept for years (remaining pictures).

If you've enjoyed a wine it's worth remembering the vintage on the label. A good vintage in one region is not necessarily good in another. The following is a general guide and should be used with care. There are always exceptions to the rule.

In good vintages Bordeaux can produce some of the greatest wines in the world. Due to modern vinification methods there has not been a really terrible vintage since 1968, and nowadays even poor vintages tend to produce very drinkable wines.
Excellent: 1983, 1982, 1978, 1975, 1970
Good: 1981, 1979, 1976, 1971
Average to poor: 1977, 1974, 1973, 1972

Burgundy is far less consistent than Bordeaux because of the large number of producers, the very varied wine-making techniques, and the climate. Thus it is very difficult to generalise and there are exceptions everywhere.
Excellent: 1983, 1978, 1971
Good: 1982, 1981, 1980, 1979, 1976, 1972, 1970

Caves Museux
1 à 45
Galeries A.B.C.D.E.
Superficie - 5527 m. 46

Right: a junior cellarman in Champagne with a stack of jeroboams. Far right: snow carpets the ground in Burgundy. Although vines can survive temperatures of -18° centigrade, a late frost can kill young shoots and ruin that year's wine.

Average to poor: 1977, 1975, 1974, 1973

The best vintages in Germany are the ones which produce a very high level of natural sugar in the grapes, allowing the producer to make the great sweet wines like Beerenauslese.
Excellent: 1983, 1976, 1975, 1971
Good: 1981, 1979
Average: 1982, 1980, 1978, 1977, 1974, 1973, 1972

Vintage port is not made every year and so each year it is 'declared' the quality will be of a relatively high level to start with.
Excellent: 1983, 1982, 1977, 1963
Good: 1980, 1975, 1970, 1966, 1960, 1958, 1955

Vintage champagne, like vintage port, is only declared in certain years, the production of the other years going into non-vintage champagne.
    The following vintages have been declared by many champagne houses in the last ten years:
1981, 1979, 1978, 1976, 1975

Opening the Bottle

Right: a selection of wine corks. Many corks are printed with information regarding the wine, and a sound cork is important for the condition of the wine. Facing page: extracting the cork with a Butler's Friend demands considerable skill and not a little strength.

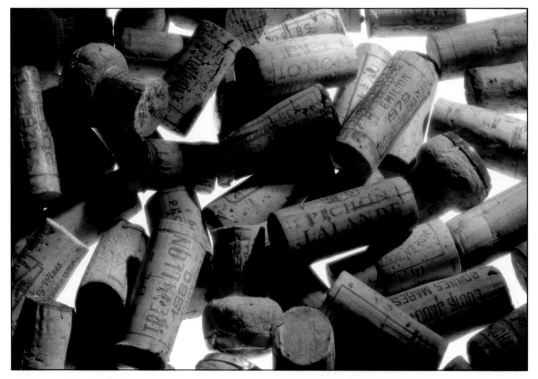

Choosing a Corkscrew

Once you've chosen the wine, the next most important thing to do is open it. First of all, remove the capsule so that it does not come into contact with the wine when poured. Lead capsules do not add an attractive flavour to the wine. Then find a corkscrew: the choice is up to you, but it should be one which you find easy to operate and, if you are going to open lots of bottles, one which is fast. For me, the best on the market is the *Screwpull*, which is fairly pricy (about £8) but rarely fails to do the job. The advantage of the Screwpull is that you do not have to be Superman to be able to use it! You merely insert the gadget into the cork, which then rides up the screw as you turn it. Virtually no strength is needed.

Most other corkscrews operate by some form of leverage – for example there are the double-armed ones which can do a reasonable job. Others, for example the *Waiter's Friend*, need considerable strength to ease the cork out. The wooden double helix corkscrews are easy to operate and quite effective, but you can't see what's happening to the cork.

The *Butler's Friend* corkscrew, a two pronged affair with no screw at all, only results in success if you are experienced in using it. Often called the 'wiggle and twist', it involves inserting the two prongs either side of the cork and gently pulling it out. It can be useful for very delicate corks but is often difficult to insert if the corks are new. You also need a fair amount of brute force for very stiff corks.

Opening Champagne Bottles

Opening champagne bottles is fun, but it can also be dangerous. You should unwrap the foil and then undo the wire, making sure that you keep your thumb over the top of the cork. Bottles that are warm, or have been shaken up, are more likely to explode. Then, with a cloth in your hand, you should hold the cork (the metal caps on the corks can be sharp), and turn the bottle not the cork. If you turn the cork it can break off. The cork should come out with a gentle pop and it's a good idea to

The corking and uncorking of champagne is a time-consuming business. After removing the sediment created by the secondary fermentation, the bottles have to be topped up (right) before new corks are fitted (below). Facing page: (top) it is best to remove the foil before undoing the wire and gently easing out the cork. Bottom right: champagne corks upon removal from the bottle and (bottom left) the relaxed state to which they will return after a few weeks.

have a glass ready to catch the first drops. If the cork is stiff (sometimes they are if the champagne is young) you can use a pair of champagne pincers to help it out.

Screw Caps

Many table wines are sold in screw-cap bottles which are, of course, the easiest to open. Generally it is wines which are meant to be consumed quite young that are packaged like this.

Wine Does not Always Come in Bottles

Over the last five years there has been a revolution in packaging. Most successful in terms of sales are bag-in-box wines. Normally three litres in size, the wine is drawn out from the box by a tap. They can be kept for up to three months before the wine deteriorates, and are useful for parties and picnics. Contrary to popular belief a bag-in-box wine is often more expensive than the equivalent amount of the same wine in a bottle. This is mainly because the packaging is so expensive. If you are only purchasing it in bulk to save

Five bottles of Minervois being opened with different corkscrews. From left to right: the wooden double-helix, which invariably works but obscures a view of the cork; the Italian double-lever, which sometimes demands a final pull by hand; the Screwpull; the Butler's Friend and the Waiter's Friend, the last two demanding some strength to operate.

SCREWPULL

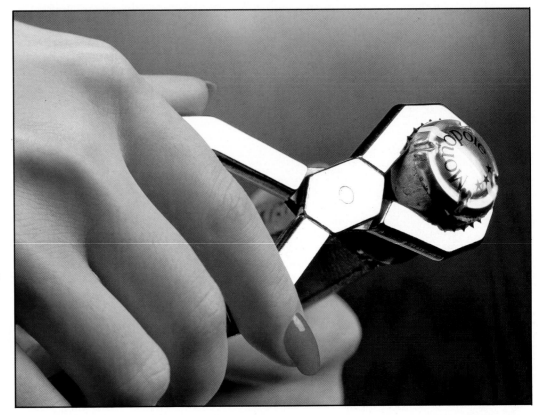

Right: some stubborn champagne corks demand the use of champagne pliers.
Below: two modern gadgets designed to keep wine fresh after it has been opened.
Below right: a can, carton and box – three modern alternatives to the bottle for storing and shipping wine.
Facing page: wine may be decanted from a box for a dinner party, to give a more elegant look.

money, check the bottle price before you buy.

Small 25cl cans are also useful, especially if you only want one glass of wine and do not want to open a bottle. They can be a good idea when cooking with wine, as recipes often only require one glass of wine.

Tetrapacks (fruit juices are also sold in them) can be useful for picnics. Cans and tetrapacks, however, should always be consumed soon after purchase and the best ones to buy are those with a 'sell by' date on them. In this way you can ensure that the wine is fresh.

Tasting Wine

Far too much mystique is attached to wine tasting. The main reason for tasting is to determine if you like the wine, just as anyone cooking would taste a sauce to see if it is to their liking. Wine tasting is fun and enjoyable and one can learn a lot from it.

When you have ten or more wines to taste – and you want to remain standing and be able to remember what the first one tasted like – it's best to spit out the wine. Some people might think this is pretentious, but in fact it is very practical. If you have visited a wine fair where hundreds of wines are on show you will know what to look for in the colour, smell and taste of the wine.

1. Colour. First you look at the colour. To do this properly you need to use clear (not coloured or cut) glass. All wine should be bright – it is not a good sign if it is cloudy. A purpley-red colour usually indicates a fairly young wine; red wine that is a browny-orange colour is an older wine.

White wines with a green tinge are usually very young and, in general, the older the white wine the deeper its yellow colour becomes. Some dessert wines,

Above: a shop sign in Chinon, France. Right: a professional wine taster with an array of wines and a spitoon. Facing page: the difference in colour between the slightly greenish Frascati from Rome and the deeper yellow Sauternes of Bordeaux indicates the greater sweetness of the latter.

know that everything quickly starts to blur if you don't spit out!

How to Taste
Professionals who can tell you the name and vintage of a wine without seeing the label are not clairvoyants. They simply

such as Sauternes, generally have a much deeper colour, and are thicker in texture. If a wine is high in alcohol (for example Sauternes or port), the wine leaves glycerine – referred to as *legs* – down the sides of the glass when swirled around. From looking at the wine you can see if it is

The colour of wine is an important indicator of quality and is best seen against a light background. Above: (left) a rosé; (centre) a Beaujolais and (right) a Bordeaux. Facing page: (top) inspecting the colour prior to smelling (bottom left) and tasting (bottom right).

still, sparkling or pétillant (slightly sparkling).

2. Smelling the wine. This is just like smelling food to see if it's fresh, or whether the scent is pleasant. You should only fill the glass one third full to do this properly. Then, without spilling the wine, gently swirl it round in the glass. This allows the smell, or *bouquet*, to develop in the glass. Then take a good sniff. You can tell instantly if food is bad or has gone off by smelling it, and the same applies to wine.

In order to get a good sniff it is important not to serve the wine in too narrow a glass. If you've a big nose you'll have trouble tasting out of a tall, thin 'copita' shaped sherry glass!

3. Tasting the wine. After smelling the wine you should then take a sip and swirl it around your mouth so that it covers all parts of the taste buds on the tongue. Then, if you're tasting a number of wines, you spit it out. There are some people in the wine trade who can spit accurately up to 20 or 30 feet. However, be warned, this is not advisable unless you're outside in the garden or have had a lot of practice!

Many wines leave a lingering flavour in the mouth after swallowing or spitting. This is referred to as the *aftertaste*.

Tasting in a Restaurant
The procedure in a restaurant is slightly different – most proprietors are not too impressed if you spit wine all over their expensive carpets!

In a good restaurant the wine waiter will show you the bottle before he opens

Above: a wine from the complicated region of Pomerol, where nearly every family produces wine and generalisations are difficult. It is usual, in a restaurant, for the waiter to show the label to the customer before opening the wine. Facing page: a selection of cheeses and fruits which go well with white wine.

be offered a taste. House wine is often a good choice if you are at a loss as to what to order, as it is usually relatively inexpensive. The main thing to remember in a restaurant is that you should drink what you want. Don't let the wine waiter frighten or bully you – it is quite possible that he knows less about wine than you do!

The following are some helpful questions (and answers) about faults in wine.

Q What does corked mean?
A This has nothing to do with bits of cork floating around in the wine. It is a mould which affects the cork and makes the wine taste and smell of cork. It can happen to any wine (at least all that are sealed with corks), from the cheapest to the most expensive. A good restaurant will change the bottle. Even if one bottle from a case is corked the other eleven may well be perfectly alright.

Bits of cork in the wine don't affect the taste, but it is best to fish them out as cork is not particularly digestible!

Q Should I send back a white wine with crystals in it?
A No. These are called *tartrates*, and do not in any way affect the flavour or taste of the wine. They are formed when the wine has undergone rapid changes in temperature.

Q I have noticed some older red wines which have had little bits in the bottom of the bottle. What causes this and how should one serve such a wine?
A This deposit is called the *sediment*, and is caused by the natural ageing of wine in the bottle. Vintage port (aged in bottle rather than cask) always has sediment in the bottle. The best thing to do with such wines is to decant them or, if that's not possible, to filter them. An easy way is to use a clean coffee filter. Young wines generally don't throw a sediment.

Sediment does not affect the taste of the wine and does not indicate a bad wine. Often, in fact, the contrary is the case.

Q What does the term 'drying out' mean?
A This is when a wine has passed its peak and the fruit is getting a little tired and dull, leaving a very bitter, dry flavour on the aftertaste. This should not be mistaken for tannin – the bitter substance (also found in tea) usually quite noticeable in young red wines.

it. It is always worth checking that it is the same wine you ordered – in particular check that it's the same vintage. It's too late to discover it is the wrong wine when the bottle is practically finished.

In most restaurants the wine waiter will pour a little wine into the glass for you to taste. Inevitably they offer it to the male, but it should be offered to whoever ordered it, male, female or otherwise! You should look at the wine to check it isn't cloudy, smell it and taste it. If you think there is something wrong with it now is the time to say – once the bottle is half empty you won't have much success in complaining.

If you order the house wine (the restaurant's ordinary wine) it is usual not to

Drinking Wine

Wine can be drunk out of almost anything, from the bottle itself to a glass slipper! As a rule of thumb, however, it is best to drink wine out of something which does not impair, or add anything to, its flavour. If you want to see the wine most clearly, glass is the ideal material. Glasses have been used for drinking wine ever since it was invented, and there are still some Roman glasses in existence.

To appreciate the exact colour of the wine to its full extent it is best to use clear, uncut and uncoloured glass.

Most wine glasses have stems. This helps you swirl the wine around the glass when tasting and also means that greasy fingerprints don't cover the glass. It is harder to swirl wine around in a tumbler – and a bottle wouldn't go very far if everyone drank out of tumblers.

There are many different shapes of glasses available, sold under various design names, many of which are largely unnecessary. Some shapes, however, are more complementary to certain types of wine.

Flutes (tall, relatively narrow glasses) are good for champagne or sparkling wine because the bubbles disappear less quickly than in a large glass, as they are not so exposed to the air. Saucer-shaped glasses are to be avoided as the wine loses its fizz quickly and if you try walking around with one in your hand you'll find you spill at least half!

In general, a tulip-shaped glass or a Paris goblet is the most versatile, and can be used for all types of wines. The size of the glass is optional, and although many restaurants serve the white wine in a

Above: the Savoy 90 cocktail, a mixture of lime juice, orangeflower water and champagne. Right: though attractive and tidy, keeping wine in the kitchen is less than ideal. The heat from cooking and washing impairs the flavour of reds and can destroy that of champagnes. Facing page: the modern way to maintain the temperature of wine.

Champagne flute. Although tricky to fill because the bubbles race to the top of the glass, the flute is ideal for champagne. The fizziness of the wine is released more slowly than in the saucer-shaped style and so the wine can be better enjoyed.

Small wine glass. A fairly standard shape which is not limited to any particular type of wine. However it is normal to serve chilled white wine in small glasses so that frequent replenishments from an ice-cooled bottle keep the wine cool and refreshing.

Large wine glass. Larger glasses are generally used for red wine, but they should not be more than a third-full at any time. This allows room for the wine to breathe, while the sloping sides capture the bouquet admirably.

Cheap pub glass. The glasses so often encountered in pubs and clubs are usually short-stemmed and made of thick glass. This makes them ideal for the rather rough treatment which they receive, but rather less than perfect for drinking wine.

Sherry copita. The copita is one of the finest wine glasses in the world. Its lines are simple and elegant, yet perfectly suited to the drinking of sherry. The long, thin shape funnels the scent of the wine into the nostrils, while it holds about the right amount for the average person.

Brandy bowl. A good quality brandy bowl should be made of the thinnest glass possible and contain little more than a splash of spirit. The bowl is then cupped in the palm of the hand and the brandy swilled around to be gently warmed. At the same time the inward-curving glass captures the heady fumes perfectly.

Although some fine Clarets, such as the bottle of Beau-Rivage (facing page), improve with careful handling, there is no point in being pretentious about wine: mixing white wine with mineral water and ice (right) produces spritzer, a cool and refreshing summer drink.

itself cause problems, since washing-up detergent can affect the taste of a wine quite considerably. When drunk from a glass which has not been properly rinsed, a sparkling wine will loss its fizz very quickly and a still wine will taste very unpleasant. It is always worth smelling the empty glass before you pour the wine into it. If it smells of dirty dishcloths or detergent you should rinse it again. After all, you want to enjoy the wine you've paid good money for!

Whatever glass designers would have us believe, it is important that you drink wine from a glass you like. It is often better to ignore the rules and simply enjoy the wine!

Decanters

Decanters can be used for any wine, although they are not advisable for sparkling wine as too much exposure to the air will make the fizz disappear rapidly.

There are two main reasons for using a decanter: to get rid of sediment and to aerate the wine. If there is sediment in the bottom of the bottle you can get rid of it by decanting the wine so that the deposit is left along the side of the bottle. You can then enjoy the wine without picking the bits from your teeth when you drink it.

When you decant a wine you allow air to get to it. Some heavy red wines like Italian Barolos benefit from this extra aeration, which can make the wine less hard and tannic. Equally, decanting some very special old wines could make them deteriorate because of too much aeration.

If you serve wine in a decanter most people will automatically assume it is an expensive wine. If you want to cheat you can serve bag-in-box wine in a decanter! It looks better, and most of your guests will think you have paid for a far better wine. Remember that the majority of people are very impressionable. You could even become a wine snob yourself!

When the wine has sediment, decanting should be done over a candle or torch so you can see through the wine. The bottle should be tilted slowly so as not to disturb the sediment. Before decanting, the bottle should be left upright so that the sediment has a chance to settle.

Serving Temperatures

All the rules about wine are there to be ignored, and the temperature at which you

smaller glass than the red this is not essential.

However, if you are going to have several wines, it helps to know which wine is in which glass. The easiest way to do this is to have different shaped or sized glasses for each wine. Brandy or liqueur glasses are generally smaller, presumably because glass manufacturers don't think we should drink too much of these! The idea behind the balloon-shaped brandy glass is to allow the glass to be easily cupped in the hand and the brandy warmed up.

Keeping glasses spotlessly clean is extremely important. If you were to put some of the same bottle of wine in a clean and in a dirty glass you would be amazed at the difference in flavour.

However, getting the glasses clean can

serve the wine is entirely up to you. If you like your white wines warm and all your red wines chilled – that's fine. If not, it is thought that white wines are at their best when slightly chilled, but beware – over-chilled white wines can lose much of their taste.

Red wines were traditionally served at room temperature, but a hundred years ago, before the advent of central heating,

sparkling wine quickly you can put it briefly, for 15-30 minutes, in the freezer, but beware – if you forget about it it is likely to explode.

If you put a bottle of wine in an ice bucket it will chill more quickly if you add water to the ice. There are also a variety of coolers available: those that hold the wine at the same temperature and those which have detachable freezer packs which cool

Right: a firm grip is often needed when pouring champagne as condensation on the cold bottle may cause it to slip. Facing page: a fine bottle of Alsace wine accompanies a prawn prepared in the fashionable *nouvelle cuisine* style.

room temperature was very much lower than it is today.

Red wines today are often served so warm that the flavour of the wine is stewed. If a red wine is very cold and you want to warm it up quickly the best way to achieve this is to put it in a bucket of hot water. Putting it in the oven or, even worse, in the microwave, is definitely *not* recommended as it will destroy the wine.

Some red wines such as Beaujolais, Chinon or Bourgueil are traditionally drunk slightly chilled.

Sparkling wines generally taste fresher and crisper when chilled, and are more refreshing served that way. To chill a

the wine very rapidly.

If a wine served in a restaurant isn't cold enough for your liking (irrespective of what the wine waiter says), ask for an ice bucket. If a wine is too cold it's more difficult. You have to tell them not to give it three seconds in the microwave! However, if you cup a glass of wine in your hands it will soon warm up.

These are only suggestions, not necessities. Always remember that it is you who is going to drink the wine, and that you are the person who should determine the temperature at which it should be drunk.

Food and Wine

Good wine is best appreciated with fine, fresh food, but can also help the preparation of such food pass more quickly for the cook (right). Facing page: light red wine such as Chenas, which has long been considered one of the best Beaujolais, is ideal with smoked salmon and other delicate foods.

People get far too worried about choosing which wines to serve with which food, and often end up drinking something they don't enjoy just because some so-called 'expert' suggested it. Food and wine are made to go with each other in whatever combination you prefer. Like all rules, those traditionally relating to food and wine are there to be broken.

Red wine can be enjoyed with fish just as a white wine can go well with red meat. More important is to match the style of wine and food. Light wines go with light food and heavy, more full-bodied wines with rich, heavier foods. It is often worthwhile matching wine and food from the same region.

Because a dry wine can taste sour after a sweet wine it is best to serve dry wines first, or throughout a meal. The same applies to ordinary and fine wines – if you serve an ordinary wine after a particularly good one, the ordinary one will seem even worse because you subconsciously compare it with the better one.

Sweet wines should be at least as sweet as the pudding, if not sweeter, otherwise all that you will taste will be the acidity.

In France, the cheese is served before the pudding, so that if you haven't finished the red wine with the main course it can be finished with the cheese. Often the best red is served with the cheese.

There are some foods, however, that don't go very well with wine because the flavour is so strong that it swamps the wine. These include highly spiced foods and curries, where lager is a sensible alternative to wine. Any food high in acidity (for example salad dressing) can make the wine taste odd.

Below are a few suggestions, but don't treat then as 'musts'. It is important to experiment to discover what you like best.

Many continental recipes call for wine as an ingredient, but it would be a great waste to use an *Appellation Contrôlée* wine for cooking. A VDQS, Vins Délimités de Qualité Supérieure, such as Minervois

from the south of France, is more than adequate for such a purpose. For drinking with oysters (facing page) and other seafood, however, a good quality white, such as Chablis, is called for.

White fish and seafood – dry white wines/
light fruity reds
Pâté/foie gras – sweet whites/Sauternes/
full-bodied reds
Pheasant/game – strong, heavy reds
Chicken – medium to full dry whites and
medium reds
Pasta – medium reds, especially Italian or
Spanish
Stews – medium to full reds
Red meat – medium to full reds
Cheese – red/port
Pudding – Sweet wines or champagne/
fortified wines

It is often a good idea to match wines with foods from the same region, such as the French cheeses (this page) and combining Fitou with Cassoulet (facing page), both from Toulouse.

The World's Wine Producers

The Loire Valley produces some fine wines in the surroundings of its fairy-tale architecture. Facing page: the chateau of Luynes, where wine is bottled in the distinctive Loire bottle (above right), a more fluted version of the Burgundy.

France

The Loire Valley

The Loire Valley is one of the most attractive regions of France. Beautiful châteaux and gardens look out over France's longest river, which flows for about 635 miles, with vineyards on either side for the last 250 miles. Many of the châteaux have been converted into hotels, which are often very reasonably priced and are set in idyllic surroundings. A number of them have huge firework displays ('Feux d'artifice') on summer evenings.

The region's food is delicious, with lots of the fresh fish and shellfish which complement the wines of the Loire so well.

The Loire Valley produces some of the best value wines available in England. Starting from the Atlantic the first region you come to is the Pays Nantais, the home of Muscadet. This is a crisp, dry white wine, available in all wine shops in England. The actual grape is called Muscadet, or Melon de Bourgogne.

There are various types of Muscadet: straight AC Muscadet and AC Muscadet de Sèvre et Maine, referring to a more specific region. Of these wines the latter, with the addition of *Sur Lie* after its name, is the best quality Muscadet available and is, therefore, more expensive than ordinary Muscadet.

Sur Lie is a French expression referring to the way the wine is made, and means

quite simply that the wine is bottled directly off its lees (the dead bits of yeast etc which are left in the wine after fermentation). This technique gives the wine the maximum amount of flavour, and means it does not have to undergo any type of filtering. The basic theory about making wine is that the less it is moved during its vinification process, the better.

Muscadet is best drunk young – usually two years old at the maximum. If it is a lot older than this and still on the shelves the chances are, except in excep-

Above: the labels of two wines from the upper Loire: Sancerre and Pouilly-Fumé. Both wines are slightly greenish in colour and smoky in flavour. Far right: the vineyards of Turckheim in Alsace.

tional circumstances, that it will taste rather lifeless.

Another wine to look out for is Muscadet Nouveau, which is a very young wine, very crisp and dry, and usually first on sale between November and December following the vintage.

Also made in this region is Gros Plant, again the name of the grape. Similar in style, this dry white wine is generally slightly cheaper than Muscadet, but is not seen so widely in Britain.

Moving upstream along the Loire the next region you come to is Anjou Saumur. A huge quantity of Anjou Rosé, a fairly dry rosé wine, is made here. It is also the main

area for the sparkling, white Saumur wine made by the *méthode champenoise* and sold in a champagne-style bottle. This is a good, dry fizz, cheaper than champagne, but with the good, crisp flavour of the Chenin Blanc grape.

Of the red wines Saumur Champigny is probably the best known. This is a light, fruity dry wine which is a pleasant summer drink when slightly chilled.

The Loire produces a number of very sweet wines too, ideal for drinking with puddings. Names to look out for include Côteaux de Layon, Bonnezeaux, Savennières and Vouvray.

Vouvray comes from Touraine, the next region upriver. It can be sparkling (like Saumur), still, sweet or dry. The important words to look out for are *sec* (dry), *demi-sec* (medium dry/sweet) and *moelleux* (sweet). Some labels, however, give no description. In this instance, you can work it out if you can vaguely remember what the weather was like during the vintage. This might sound incredibly complicated but it isn't!

Below: one of many roadside signs in France proclaiming the pedigree of the local wine, which can usually be sampled nearby.

As a general rule, years with a lot of sunshine like 1976 or 1982 produce wines which will tend to be sweeter than those made after poor summers. Vouvray, unlike Muscadet, can keep for several years, and I've tasted some which were as much as 60 years old.

Red wines from Touraine include Chinon and Bourgueil; fruity, quite earthy in taste, dry wines which often smell and

taste of raspberries and strawberries.

The vineyards furthest up the Loire Valley are referred to as the central vineyards. This is where Sancerre and Pouilly-Fumé (not to be confused with Pouilly-Fuissé, a white burgundy) are made. Made from the Sauvignon grape, they are crisp, dry white wines with more depth than Muscadet, and generally rather more expensive. If you're visiting the region, Sancerre is a fascinating place to go to: an ancient, walled town, high on the top of a hill surrounded by vineyard slopes.

Below: a monument to the monk who became the father of champagne and one of the great figures in the history of wine. Right: a selection of champagne bottles and gift sets. Bottom: the tricky process of *dégorgement*, in which the sediment is removed from the bottle. Facing page: a map showing the first-class, and other, wine producing regions of France.

Champagne

Champagne, the drink everyone associates with success and happy occasions, is produced in one of France's most northerly vineyards.

Champagne has a long history, and many people attribute its invention to a monk named Dom Perignon. Legend has it that he was the man who discovered how to keep the bubbles in champagne.

The region of Champagne is relatively small (only 86,000 acres) and by law the only wine in the world that can legally carry the name 'champagne' is the sparkling wine made in this region by the *méthode champenoise*. Other sparkling wines, even those from France, California, Spain or anywhere else in the world made by the same method are not champagne.

Because the region is quite small and the process involved very complicated and labour-intensive, champagne has always been relatively expensive.

The bubbles in champagne are

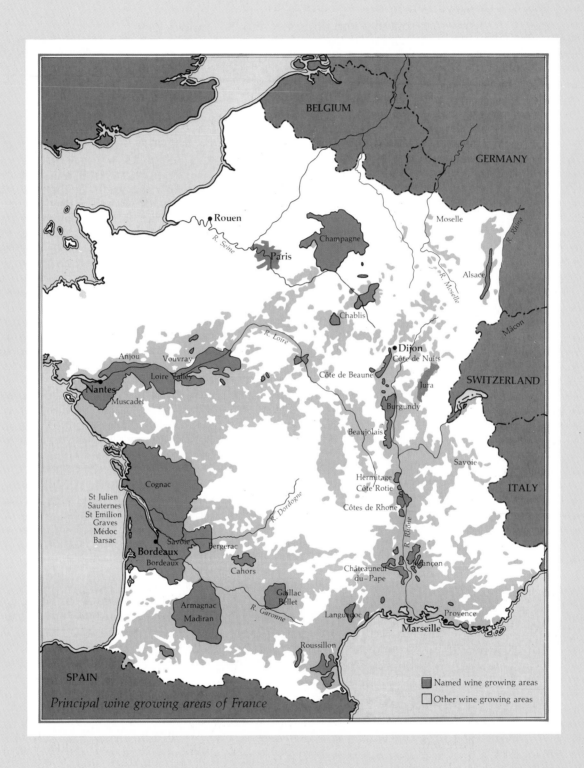

BELGIUM

GERMANY

R. Seine

Rouen

R. Rhine

Moselle

Champagne

Paris

Alsace

R. Moselle

Chablis

R. Loire

Mâcon

Anjou

Vouvray

Dijon

Côte de Nuits

Loire Valley

Côte de Beaune

Nantes

Jura

SWITZERLAND

Muscadet

Burgundy

Beaujolais

Savoie

Cognac

Hermitage
Côte Rôtie

ITALY

St Julien
Sauternes
St Emilion
Graves
Médoc
Barsac

R. Dordogne

Côtes de Rhone

Savoie

Bergerac

Bordeaux

R. Rhône

Bordeaux

Ancon

Cahors

Châteauneuf
du-Pape

Gaillac
Bellet

Armagnac
Madiran

R. Garonne

Languedoc

Provence

Marseille

Roussillon

SPAIN

Named wine growing areas

Principal wine growing areas of France

Other wine growing areas

65

produced naturally, and the making process does not involve carbonating (inserting) bubbles into the wine. After a first fermentation in the vat, yeasts are added to the wine when it is in bottle. This causes a second fermentation in the bottle. As a result, the wine is sparkling but contains some sediment from the dead yeasts.

To get rid of this the bottles are tilted neck down and periodically shaken (*remuage*) so that the sediment collects near the neck. The neck of the bottle is then frozen, and the ice plug containing the sediment shot out of the bottle. Because of the pressure of gas inside the champagne bottle special corks are used, secured with wire. Care must be taken when opening champagne bottles, as they are likely to explode.

Champagne is made from three grapes: Chardonnay, a white grape, and two black grapes – Pinot Noir and Pinot Meunier. Although the last two are black grapes their juice is white, like that of most black grapes. To make rosé, champagne producers either leave the red skins together with the wine for between one and two days until they achieve the desired colour, or they add red wine.

Most non-vintage champagne is a blend of these grapes from different years, and is generally sold under a brand name such as Möet & Chandon, Bollinger or Lanson.

Vintage champagne, when a year is shown on the label, is the wine from one single year. It is more expensive than the blended non-vintage variety, and is only made in very good years. In general, a vintage champagne will keep far longer than a non-vintage one.

The words 'blanc de blancs' on the label means that the champagne is made from 100% white grapes. Most champagnes are 'Brut', meaning 'dry', and those called 'Ultra Brut' are extra dry, ideal for diabetics or slimmers (as they have less sugar added to them) although I've yet to see champagne included in any diet!

Burgundy

Burgundy, on the east side of France, is, like Bordeaux, one of France's classic great wine regions. It stretches from Chablis, in the north, to Beaujolais in the south. In between the two there are many different styles of wine. In Burgundy, more than any other wine region, the winemaker is very important.

Because the name Burgundy has become so famous internationally, prices have escalated and many Burgundies are now expensive. There are, however, some areas left which can offer value for money. These include (going north to south) St Bris, Haut Côte de Nuits, Haut Côte de Beaune, Côte Chalonnaise, Mâconnais and Beaujolais.

The red wines of Burgundy in general are fruitier, less tannic and lighter than the wines of Bordeaux or the Rhône. The whites (made from the Chardonnay grape) can be rich and are dry, but not as aggressively dry as most Loire whites.

Burgundy is divided up into hundreds of small vineyards. This means that in the village of Gevrey-Chambertin alone there are numerous different growers, all of whom make a different style of wine. If you enjoy a bottle of burgundy it's definitely worth remembering the grower's name.

Beaujolais red wines are made from the Gamay grape (all other Burgundy reds are made from Pinot Noir). Don't judge the region by Beaujolais Nouveau – there are in fact some delicious wines to be found, particularly from the nine Beaujolais villages listed in the Table.

Because Burgundy is such a confusing region with so many wines I have listed area by area, from north to south, the most commonly-found wines, together with their colour and style.

The Côtes-du-Rhône

The Côtes-du-Rhône region runs from Vienne in the north, downriver from Beaujolais, to Avignon in the south, just above Provence. It is split into two distinct regions, the Northern Rhône, going south as far as Valence, and the Southern Rhône, which starts at Montelimar and runs down to Avignon.

The Northern Rhône produces the fullest, heaviest wines, the best of which are now highly sought after and consequently not cheap! The best red wines include Côte-Rôtie, Hermitage, Crozes-Hermitage and Cornas and an excellent sparkling wine is made at St Peray. There are also two world-famous white wines, Condrieu and Château Grillet. The latter, which is owned by only

Facing page: rarely exported, but drunk in large quantities by locals, is the *Vin de Pays*. This classification ranks below VDQS but above Vin de Table and includes many very drinkable wines.

one proprietor, has the distinction of being the smallest Appellation in France.

AC Côtes-du-Rhône is the basic wine made in the region and is mainly produced in the Southern Rhône. It is a red wine (although you can find white Côtes-du-Rhône) which has a purpley red colour, and is fruity with a peppery flavour. It is not as dry as claret. The Southern Rhône produces somewhat lighter and jammier wines than the cooler Northern Rhône.

Three famous wine labels: (above and right) two of the finest wines from the Côte de Beaune and (above right) a fine wine from the banks of the Rhone. Facing page: pruning vines in Burgundy. Most of the prunings will be burnt, but some may later be used for grafting.

The best known of these is Châteauneuf-du-Pape, made from a mixture of up to thirteen different grape varieties. White Châteauneuf-du-Pape is also produced, but because of the hot climate the white wines tend to lack acidity. Apart from basic Côtes-du-Rhône, good value wines from the Southern Rhône include Gigondas, Vacqueyras, Côtes du Ventoux and Côteaux de Tricastin. There are also some very good dry, full-bodied rosés made in Lirac and Tavel.

My personal favourite from the Southern Rhône is a sweet dessert wine called Muscat de Beaumes-de-Venise. Made from the strongly-perfumed Muscat grape, this luscious wine is pinky-gold in colour, honeyed on the nose and

deliciously sweet and rich. It is high in alcohol and is classed as a 'fortified' wine meaning, that grape spirit has been added to the wine during its vinification. It goes especially well with raspberries and Christmas pudding. When served chilled it is easy to drink too much of it!

Bordeaux

For most connoisseurs bordeaux is the ultimate wine. In many ways that's because of tradition – in the 18th century *clairet*, now known as claret, was the gentleman's only drink. Many other

countries have tried to imitate Bordeaux's wines by planting the same grape varieties, especially California and Australia. To this day, however, Bordeaux still leads the wine market, and arguably makes the finest wines in the world.

The main regions of Bordeaux are divided by two rivers, the Gironde and the Dordogne, whose confluence, the Garonne, runs into the Atlantic. On the left of the Gironde and Garonne are the Médoc and Graves, and on the right bank of the Dordogne are Saint Emilion and Pomerol.

In Bordeaux the wines are known by the name of the château (French for house or castle); these vary in size from huge castle-like buildings to tiny shack-like houses. The basic Appellation is AC Bordeaux, and the next one up AC Bordeaux Supérieur.

The top wines of Bordeaux are called *Crus Classés* (or Classed Growths) and are graded from First Growth through to Fifth Growth, following a classification in 1855. The First Growths are rated to be amongst the world's greatest wines, and this is reflected in their price.

There are only five First Growths – Châteaux Latour, Lafite-Rothschild, Margaux and Mouton-Rothschild in the Médoc and, in Graves, Château Haut-Brion. There are also two in St Emilion – Châteaux Ausone and Cheval-Blanc – and one in Pomerol – Château Petrus. Whilst delicious, these wines are very expensive and are often bought more because of the name on the label than for their taste. Below the Classed Growths are Cru Bourgeois wines – these often represent the best value for money in Bordeaux.

Claret, always red in colour, is a dry, fairly tannic wine. Many of the Classed Growths and the better Cru Bourgeois age their wines in oak barrels called *barriques*. The oak, together with the grape skins which are left in contact with the wine, produce the tannin, a bitter substance that makes the wines hard and unpleasant to taste when young, but enables them to last for a long time.

Three main grape varieties are used in claret: Cabernet Sauvignon, Cabernet Franc and Merlot. They are blended together in different proportions, determined by the winemaker and by how much of each grape variety the château has planted in its vineyards. In the Médoc the Cabernet Sauvignon is predominant, whilst Merlot is the main variety used across the river in Saint Emilion and Pomerol. This leads to different styles of wine. Médoc and Graves clarets tend to be more austere, powerful and longer lived than the more delicate, softer wines of Saint Emilion and Pomerol.

Many people don't realise how much white wine is produced in the Bordeaux region. This is where Entre-deux-Mers (the region between the rivers Dordogne and

Above left: the label of one of the finest wines of Bordeaux, the vineyards being located in the southern suburbs of the city. Above right: the label of an Alsace wine bottled for one of the more respected shippers. Facing page: an unusual bottle holder containing wine from Sancerre.

Gironde) comes from, a crisp, dry white wine made mainly from a grape called Sauvignon.

The other white wine for which Bordeaux is famous is Sauternes. This is a rich, luscious, sweet wine, high in alcohol and often referred to as a dessert wine. Sauternes is a very difficult wine to make. The producer leaves the Sauvignon and Semillon grapes on the vines long after the grapes from the rest of the region have been picked. The grapes shrivel up, go a browny-yellow colour and are affected by a noble rot called *botrytis cinerea*. If successfully attacked by this rot, the shrivelled grapes are eventually harvested in October/November, the pickers often selecting individual grapes from the bunches. By this stage the grapes are very high in sugar levels and the resulting wine, deep gold in colour, is rich and sweet.

Making Sauternes is a risky business, because at any time whilst the grapes are left rotting they could be destroyed by bad weather. Because of this complicated process genuine Sauternes is expensive.

The wine industry of France preserves many traditional methods including: (left) horse-drawn transport, (top) hand picking and (above) wooden grape carriers.

The Rest of France

Under this wide-ranging heading there are literally hundreds of wines from which to choose; almost every tiny village in France grows some vines. When on holiday in France it is always worth trying the local wine, even if you've never heard of it. Often the smaller or less known the village, the more eager the locals will be for you to try their wines.

Some areas of France that are becoming more and more popular in this

country are in the south and south-west of France. Names to watch out for are Languedoc, Rousillon, Minervois, Cahors, Jurançon, Provence, Madiran and Buzet, amongst others. These are generally full-bodied, fruity red wines, and can be very good value for money.

For white wine drinkers Alsace is an important region. Once part of Germany, this region produces very spicy, dry white wines, in many ways more German than French in style, although heavier and more powerful in flavour. This is where the flowery, spicy Gewürztraminer grape is at its best. All Alsace wines (sometimes called Alsatian, although I always thought that was a dog!) are named after the grape variety from which they are made, and the

Left: an array of better-known labels from the Sancerre region of the Loire Valley. Above: estate workers in Beaujolais sample the current year's *nouveau* before it is shipped to a waiting world.

majority of them are white. Seven basic grapes are used, of which Riesling is the most common, making a full-bodied dry wine.

Other grapes commonly used in Alsace include Pinot Gris, often, rather confusingly, called Tokay d'Alsace, again producing a dry wine. The sweet wines of Alsace are made from grapes which have been 'late-picked' (Vendange Tardive) and are, consequently, high in sugar content. Delicious though these wines are, they are generally quite expensive.

Another name you'll see quite often on labels is 'Edelzwicker', which means a blend of grape varieties.

Pinot Noir, the grape of Burgundy, is used to make both red and rosé wines in Alsace, although it is often difficult to tell the difference between the two! Reds and rosés from Alsace are not widely available in Britain.

Alsace wines are easily recognisable by their tall, thin, German-style bottles.

Germany

Most wine drinkers start by drinking German wines. This is probably because they are light, low-in-alcohol, fruity, flowery, often medium-sweet wines which are easy to drink, pleasant and rarely offensive.

Bottled in their distinctive, long-necked bottles, German wines are easily recognisable on a supermarket shelf. This is probably just as well because, apart from a few well-known brand names, the names on the labels are generally unpronounceable!

The labels may often look indecipherable, but don't be put off – they are generally quite logical, even if the ones written in flowery Gothic script are often impossible to read!

German wines come in two different coloured bottles, brown glass for hock, (Rhine wines) and green glass for wines from the Mosel.

Much wine that on initial appearances seems to be German is really an EEC blend – made in Germany but using a mixture of grapes from other countries (in particular Italy), and blended to produce a 'Germanic' style of wine.

The basic level of German wine is called Tafelwein (table wine), often

prefixed by the word Deutscher, meaning German.

A fairly recent introduction is Landwein – similar to a French vin de pays. Above this are QbA wines (Qualitätswein bestimmte Anbaugebiete), meaning quality wine from a designated region. These words cover a wide range of wines from the different regions.

In many ways it is surprising that vines prosper in Germany, as it is one of the most northerly vineyard regions in Europe. Much research has been done over the years to develop hardy grape varieties which can survive the low temperatures. The main variety used is the Riesling (pronounced Reece-ling), which has been crossed with another variety, the Sylvaner, to produce Müller-Thurgau. This is now the predominant grape variety in Germany and has the advantage of ripening early and producing a huge crop. Whilst Müller-Thurgau is used in the QbA wines such as Niersteiner or Liebfraumilch, the finest QmP wines are generally made from pure Riesling.

The top category is QmP wine – Qualitätswein mit Prädikat – meaning good quality wine with a special attribute. Within this section are various styles of wines grouped according to potential alcohol and sweetness, starting with the driest, Kabinett, then (in ascending order of sweetness) Spätlese, Auslese, Beerenauslese and Trockenbeerenauslese. In exceptional years Eiswein (literally, 'icewine') is produced. It is made from grapes which, once ripe, are left on the vine until December and are picked at sub-zero temperatures. Because Eiswein is so difficult to make, and because the mature grapes can be damaged by hail, excess rain, etc at any time, it is normally extremely expensive.

German wines are classified according to their region of origin – many by the names of rivers near which they are produced.

The Mosel is probably the best-known river. The wines are generally labelled as Mosel-Saar-Ruwer, thus including the Mosel's two tributaries. The top wines are made from the Riesling, grown on the best south-facing slopes, whilst the more well-known wines are made from blends using a lot of Müller-Thurgau. Amongst these are Moselblümchen, Bereich Bernkastel and

Facing page: Mannenburg, a typical wine-producing town on the Mosel, with its riverside buildings and vineyards climbing the hillside beyond.

Above: the massive castle of Cochem, which dominates the vineyards on this stretch of the lower Mosel. Right: the vine-crowded slopes of a side valley off the Rhine at Assmannshausen, in the Rheingau. Facing page: a map showing the principal wine regions of Germany.

Piesport – the name of the village the wine comes from. These wines are generally fairly low in alcohol.

The Rheingau produces some of Germany's best wines from the well-known villages along the right hand side of the Rhine, where the vines face due south. Generally, the sweeter QmP wines, where the grapes are picked late, are made in this area from the Riesling grape. The best wines come from individual villages such as Erbach, Oestrich and Rüdesheim.

The vast majority of Liebfraumilch comes from the Rheinhessen, although originally it was made in a tiny village called Worms. It is made mainly from the Müller-Thurgau, with other grapes blended-in to make soft, flowery, sometimes bland wines.

Niersteiner also comes from this area. A few years ago Liebfraumilch used to be medium-sweet in style, but has now changed due to the recent demand for slightly drier wines. However, even when

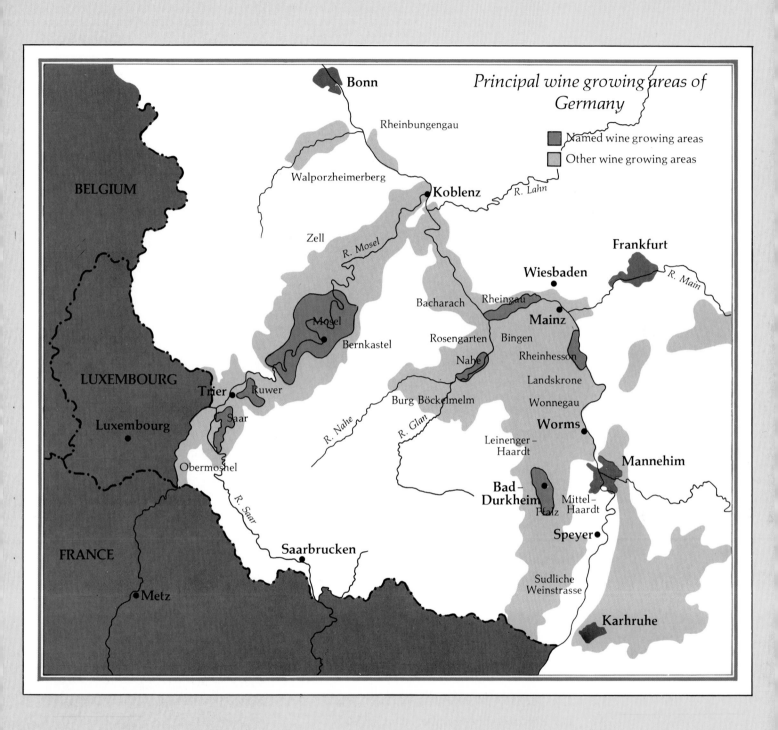

Principal wine growing areas of Germany

Named wine growing areas
Other wine growing areas

BELGIUM

LUXEMBOURG

Luxembourg

FRANCE

Metz

Bonn

Rheinbungengau

Walporzheimerberg

Koblenz

R. Lahn

Zell

R. Mosel

Frankfurt

R. Main

Wiesbaden

Bacharach

Rheingau

Mosel

Mainz

Bernkastel

Rosengarten

Bingen

Nahe

Rheinhessen

Trier

Ruwer

Landskrone

Saar

Burg Böckelmelm

Wonnegau

R. Nahe

R. Glan

Worms

Obermoshel

Leinenger –
Haardt

Mannehim

R. Saar

Bad-
Durkheim

Mittel –
Haardt

Pfalz

Speyer

Saarbrucken

Sudliche
Weinstrasse

Karhruhe

slightly dry, Liebfraumilch is nowhere near as acidic or as bone-dry as the white wines from the Loire.

Rheinpfalz (also known as the Palatinate) produces rich, flowery, spicy wines. This is not surprising when you realise it is really a continuation of Alsace, now in France, which produces wines with some of the same characteristics. Some fine German wines are made in this region.

Above: the delicate white wines of Germany are produced from such grapes as these. Right: the vine-covered slopes and traditional architecture of Beilstein, on the lower Mosel.

There are several other regions whose wines can only be found in specialist German wine shops because they are not exported in large quantities. The regions include Ahr, Franconia (the bottle is a distinctive flat flask shape), Württemberg and Baden.

Other words to look out for on German wine labels are *trocken* (meaning dry) or *halbtrocken* (meaning, literally, half dry). This tells you what style of wine to expect, but should not be confused with *Trockenbeerenauslese*, which is one of the best quality QmP wines and, far from being dry, is very rich and sweet.

Although Germany produces red and rosé wines they are not commonly seen, and are mainly interesting as a novelty rather than value-for-money. Often rather pale in colour, it's sometimes difficult to tell the difference between a red and a rosé. Unlike many red wines they are slightly sweet and without much body.

With Germany, as with any other country, it is only really by tasting different wines that you'll find what you like. Some

of the wines are commercial and, once you have acquired a taste for them, become a little bland. That's the time to experiment with a different wine. If you remember some of the words on the label, for example the region, sweetness (e.g. *Kabinett, Spätlese* etc), and/or the grape variety, you will get an idea of what is to your taste. At least that way you can eliminate those you don't like from the mass of labels and wines on offer.

Italy

Below: the monastery of St. Hidegard is surrounded by some of the highest-growing vines in the Rheingau. Facing page: an isolated chapel stands amid the vines which produce the famous Bernkastel Doktor wines of the middle Mosel.

In terms of production and per capita consumption, Italy produces and drinks the most wine per year. People tend to think of all Italian wine as cheap holiday plonk but, because of the sheer size and number of areas producing wine in Italy, this is far from the truth. There are several

hundred quality wines produced in Italy, generally found with the letters DOC and DOCG on the labels, the Italian equivalent of the French Appellation Contrôlée.

Wines from Italy can be rather confusing as they are allowed to take their name either from the region, the grape variety or the style of wine, and sometimes a mixture of all three! The same name often refers to both red and white wines. However, it is always worth considering Italy, as her finest wines are comparatively cheap by French standards.

Probably the most important quality wine-producing region is Piedmont in north-west Italy. It is a beautiful region to visit, and produces Barolo, often referred to as the king of all Italian wines. It is a deep-coloured, dry red wine which can last for many years and is often at its best after ten to fifteen years in bottle.

Barolo is aged in oak and, when young, like the young red wines of Bordeaux, is very tannic and leaves a bitter flavour in the mouth. It is this tannin, however, that enables the wine to last. Barolo is made from the Nebbiolo grape and is always a red wine.

Barbaresco also comes from Piedmont. Aged in wood, this is generally a slightly lighter wine, velvety and dry, and made from the same grape, the Nebbiolo. Another wine whose name begins with 'B', this time named after the grape variety, is Barbera. It is more pinky-red in colour and slightly lighter in style.

The best-known white wine made in this region is Italy's biggest-selling sparkler, Asti Spumante. Production is centred around the town of Asti, from which the wine takes its name. Made from the Moscato grape, Asti is usually sweet. It is made by a less expensive method than champagne, which does not involve the hours of work involved in the *remuage* (manually turning the bottles in their racks).

Another area producing some of Italy's best wines is Tuscany, the home of Chianti. This wine is made from a mixture of grapes, mainly the Sangiovese.

Amongst the white wines of Italy, apart from the sparkling Asti, Frascati (pronounced Frass-car-tee) and Soave (pronounced Swarvay) are probably the best known. They are both crisp, dry white wines, with lots of fruit, and the best examples are good value for money. Verdicchio (pronounced Ver-deek-eeo) is another wine made in the same style.

One of Italy's more recent success stories is Lambrusco. This is a sparkling wine made in Emilia-Romagna, south-east of Milan. When exported it is usually pink or red and is often *amabile* or semi-sweet. It is generally drunk chilled.

With such a wide range of Italian wines on the market the best thing to do is to buy them and taste them. Write down the names of the ones you like, noting the type of wine and district. Enjoy experimenting!

Portugal

Portugal, a country famous for its beautiful beaches, is the home of one of Britain's oldest established 'gentleman's' drinks – port.

Port came into being almost by accident. After the British Government had fallen out with the French in the late 17th century they had to go elsewhere for their red wine supplies. Bringing the dry red wine of Portugal over to England meant a lengthy sea journey, and to help stabilise the wine some brandy was added. Reports went back to Portugal that the British approved of this style of wine, so the technique was developed one stage further and brandy was added to stop the fermentation of the wine, resulting in a fairly sweet, alcoholic wine similar to today's port. Port is therefore a 'fortified' wine, like sherry, with at least half as much alcohol again as wine.

There are many different types of port resulting from different grades of grape and the varied techniques used in its production. The most widely available

Right: an armed horseman guards the chalky vineyards around Jerez, Spain, from which sherry is produced.
Below: a *barco rabelo* loaded with barrels of port for its journey down the Duoro to Oporto, Portugal.

Above: in the more remote valleys of Portugal methods are more traditional than elsewhere in Europe.

type is Ruby Port, named after its colour, which is rich and sweet.

Tawny Port is made by leaving the wine a long time in cask so it loses the brilliant deep red colour of freshly pressed juice and turns a 'tawny' colour. Often the label shows an age, such as ten, twenty, thirty, or over forty years old. Generally speaking the older the wine the higher the price will be.

However, Tawny Port with an indication of age, for example 'over 40 years of age', should not be mistaken for Vintage Port. The latter is a wine made from the finest grapes from one selected year. Rather than being aged in cask, Vintage Port is bottled when two years old and then needs many years in bottle before it is ready to drink. Unlike Tawny Port, which is matured in cask, Vintage Port throws a sediment during its maturation in the bottle and consequently needs careful decanting.

Vintage Character Port is a good quality Ruby Port and is often good value for money.

Late-bottled vintage (LBV for short) is wine from one vintage, bottled four to six years after the harvest. These ports are ready for drinking much earlier than Vintage Ports and, because they spend more time in cask, they do not need decanting.

'Crusting Port' is a cheaper alternative to Vintage Port and is a blend of wines which is matured in bottle and deposits a 'crust' (or sediment) and, therefore, needs decanting.

White Port, drunk in large quantities in both Portugal and France, is golden yellow in colour, and can be dry or sweet. It is usually drunk as an aperitif.

Portugal's Other Wines

Much the biggest production in Portugal is of table wines. The best known in England is probably Vinho Verde (Vee-no ver-day). In general only the white Vinho Verdes find their way to England, but there are many reds produced in this area, which is in the north of Portugal.

The whites are easy-to-drink, crisp wines, slightly pétillant (fizzy) as a result of carbonation. There are various theories as to how Vinho Verde, meaning green wine, got its name. Maybe it was because of the luscious green area the grapes were grown in, or the acidic, or 'green', style of the wine. What is certain is that it does not refer to unripe grapes – the grapes are always fully ripe when picked.

Of Portugal's other wines, Dão (pronounced dow) wines are probably the best value. These are full-bodied, dry red wines which are excellent value for money and can last a long time. Portugal also produces a delicious, thick, sweet white wine from the Setubal Peninsula, called Moscatel, an alcoholic dessert wine.

Portugal's most famous wines, if not its most serious, are rosés like the well-known Mateus Rosé. These are generally medium-sweet in flavour and have a slight sparkle.

Madeira

Madeira is a fascinating island to visit. Only 36 miles long and 14 miles wide, it has dramatically-steep cliffs, hot, terraced hillsides and cooler shaded valleys. Vines flourish everywhere. Halfway down steep cliff sides, which look extremely treacherous, small groups of vines grow on outcrops. In many ways the island of Madeira seems to have stood still in time and, because of the very steep, terraced vineyards, ploughing is still done manually.

Madeira, like port and sherry, is a fortified wine, which means grape spirit is added to the wine. Madeira, however, is made by an unusual method of heating the wine in an *estufa*, a large, heated store.

There are four distinctive styles of Madeira, varying from very full and sweet, to very dry wines. Named after grape varieties, these styles will be indicated on the label.

Sercial is the driest Madeira, often drunk chilled as an aperitif, and lighter in style than the sweeter Madeiras.

Verdelho is a slightly sweeter wine with a dry finish. This is the style of Madeira the Victorians used to drink with a slice of cake.

Bual is a much sweeter, richer wine for drinking with puddings.

Malmsey is the sweetest Madeira, a rich, luscious, very full wine which makes a welcome change from brandy or port after a meal.

This page: *barco rabelos* on the upper Duoro. This method of transporting port to the sea has been largely replaced by rail.

Spain

Spain's 'plonk' image is gradually changing. It is true that much Spanish wine is very cheap but, fortunately for us, it is in many cases considerably better than plonk.

Long before the Costa Brava became popular as a holiday resort Britain had been importing a wine from Southern Spain – sherry. This is a fortified wine, which means its strength is increased by the addition of brandy or spirit. Many people are unclear as to what a fortified wine is – a recent example was a girl who worked for a brewery and listed all the 'châteaux' wines under the 'fortified' wine section.

Just as real champagne comes from the region of the same name in France, so real sherry comes from Jerez (pronounced Herr-eth) in Spain.

Because they are fortified, most sherries are half as strong again as wine. Sherry, which makes an excellent aperitif when chilled and is delicious with fish

soups, comes in a variety of styles: *Fino*, generally pale in colour and dry; *Manzanilla*, slightly more bitter than Fino; *Amontillado*, amber in colour with a medium dry almondy taste; *Olorosso*, which can be sweet or dry, and *Cream Sherry*, which is rich and sweet.

Other countries, such as South Africa, Cyprus and California, produce wines similar in style to sherry. There is also 'British Sherry', not made from 'British' grapes, but from imported grape musts which are then made into 'Sherry' in Britain. None of these have quite the finesse of a true Spanish sherry.

One of the most enjoyable bi-products of sherry is sherry vinegar, delicious when used in salad dressings and always worth stocking up with when you're in Spain.

As well as sherry, Spain produces many excellent, non-fortified wines. Rioja (pronounced Ree-ock-a) has become very popular in Britain during the last ten years.

The red wines of Rioja are soft, round

Below: a typical small family holding in rural Portugal with its stone house and terraced fields.

wines, with a slightly woody taste. This taste, which adds to the complexity of the wine, giving it a vanilla-scented bouquet, is the result of ageing the wine in wooden barriques – 225 litre barrels. Rioja has many historical links with Bordeaux, and has the Bordelaise to thank for the introduction of wooden barrels.

Red Rioja is made from a variety of grapes, mainly Tempranillo, Garnacha, Mazuelo and Graciano, whilst the white is made from Viura, Malvasia and Garnacha.

The countryside in Rioja is impressive and the landscape quite severe. With its red-orange soil, it has a sunbaked, arid appearance. Grapes used in Rioja come from three areas: Rioja Baja, the hottest region producing wines high in alcohol, deep in colour and ideal for blending; Rioja Alta, wines with good fruit and consistent colour, and Rioja Alavesa, producing more delicate wines with more finesse. The best Riojas are made by blending wines from all three regions.

In Spain, the different companies are known as *bodegas* – the Spanish for cellars. The name of the bodega always features on the label. Most Riojas also have a back label, giving details about the wine's age. *Gran Reserve* is the oldest, then *Reserva*, followed by *Crianza*. *Sin Crianza* is a young wine.

Good Riojas can last for many years and, because they are continually moved from barrel to barrel during ageing and the lees (sediment) is left in the empty barrels, you don't need to decant them.

There are two distinct styles of white Rioja: *Reservas*, deep gold in colour, rich and dry with the smell and flavour of the oak in which they were aged, and wines with no classification, which are light, crisp, dry and fruity and which should be drunk within two years of the vintage on the label. The latter are a relatively modern development.

Now that Rioja has established itself as a good quality Spanish wine, a newcomer has recently come onto the market, hoping to repeat Rioja's success story. This is the region of Navarra, to the north of Rioja, which produces similar wines, although somewhat lighter and less concentrated.

Here, production is centred around the ancient town of Olite. It is a fascinating region to visit and you can even stay in the 15th century castle in Olite, which is a

parador (government owned hotel, normally housed in a historic building) and is very reasonably priced and comfortable.

Navarra red and white wines are gradually finding their way into shops and supermarkets in Britain and are generally somewhat cheaper than Rioja wines. They are excellent value for money, far more so than many Spanish table wines which don't mention their region or origin.

La Mancha, a vast wine producing area in central Spain which used to produce fairly rough white wines, has recently been improving its wine making, and now produces crisp, dry white wines.

In Penedés, which is near the tourist track just south of Barcelona, many French grape varieties have been planted. The pioneer is Miguel Torres, whose wines, both red and white, are widely available in Britain and are of sound quality. Although more expensive than the average Spanish wine, they are well worth the extra money.

The Rest of Europe

England

Many people don't realise that vines have been grown in England since Roman times, when there were extensive plantings, nor that after this period the monasteries took over the upkeep of many of the vineyards. After the Dissolution of the monasteries, vines disappeared for a few hundred years until the early 1950s. However, since then there has been a resurgence of interest, and today over 1,000 acres are under vine, with vineyards planted as far north as Lincolnshire. The majority, however, are situated in the milder climate of the south of England, especially in the counties of Kent and Sussex.

It is important not to confuse English wine with British wine. The latter can be something of a consumer 'con', as the only connection it has with Britain is that imported grape musts, usually from Cyprus or Italy, are brought to this country and made into a wine which is often fortified. The commercial logic of this is that imported grape musts from countries with a warmer climate are much cheaper than home grown grapes. English wine, however, is made from grapes grown in England. Because of England's northerly position and relatively cool climate, vine cultivation is extremely difficult and

Facing page: great stacks of wooden barrels containing maturing Californian wine.

producing grapes of decent quality requires a lot of skill. When the weather is particularly bad English wine growers sometimes harvest no grapes at all.

English wine growers not only have to battle against the elements, they also have to contend with the high government taxation. English wine is taxed at exactly the same rate as imported European wines, where production costs are lower. It is not surprising, therefore, that English wines seem relatively expensive.

Those patriotic enough to drink them, however, will not be disappointed. Techniques have greatly improved over the last few years and, with the introduction of the E.V.A. (English Vineyards Association) seal, there are some excellent white wines being made. As yet English wines have no official classification (the EEC only allows them to be called table wine) but it is well worth looking out for the ones with the E.V.A. seal. Although a few brave producers have tried producing red wines, the results

such as Chardonnay have been far less successful.

The white wines produced are either fairly dry, similar to the crisp, dry wines of the Loire Valley, or medium sweet, and more Germanic in style.

Switzerland

Many people are surprised that Switzerland, with such a high snowfall, can grow vines. Vines are generally planted on south facing slopes to gain maximum sunlight.

The wines are usually quite light, dry and delicate, the whites being made mainly from the Chasselas grape. Reds, which are normally rather thin, are made from the Pinot or Gamay grape. Although some fine wines are produced, they are largely consumed in Switzerland and those that reach this country tend to be fairly expensive. Some of the best wines are produced around Dôle.

Right: the productive vineyards north of Stellenbosch in South Africa. Some grapes, such as those (facing page top) at Wentworth in Australia, are laid out in the sun to reduce their water content before pressing and fermentation. Facing page bottom: scenes from harvest time in France, when everyone available helps with the grape picking.

suggest that England is better off sticking to whites.

German grape varieties are usually favoured as they have to survive a similar type of climate. The Müller-Thurgau, Germany's most widely planted grape, seems to flourish in English vineyards, whilst experiments with French varieties

Austria

Austrian wines are similar to German wines, but with a little more depth and richness. The main white grape is the Grüner Veltliner which produces dry whites, whilst *Schluck*, produced near Austria's famous Danube River, is sweeter.

Another widely-grown grape is the Welschriesling.

Because Austria enjoys so much more sunshine than Germany, it produces mostly rich, sweet wines, expecially in Burgenland, where the weather encourages noble rot, producing wines with a high 'natural sugar content like Sauternes and Beerenauslese.

In the past, much of Austria's wine was drunk locally without being bottled, but now the producers realise its potential and more and more is being bottled and exported.

Eastern Europe

Hungary

Hungary's most famous wine is Tokay, a sweet wine matured in barrels called *gonci*, and sweetened by adding *puttonyos* (tubs) of concentrated grape juice called *aszu*. The more puttonyos added, the sweeter the wine. The best Tokay can last for centuries.

You can now find a Tokay also called *Szamorodni*, which tastes more like a dry sherry.

Hungary's most widely-known wine is Bull's Blood, a dry, deeply coloured red wine from the town of Eger. Although rarely left for long in bottle, Bull's Blood can keep for a considerable time.

Hungary is now developing more and more dry white wine, which is gradually becoming available in Britain.

Yugoslavia

Yugoslavia's best known wine is the Laski Riesling (pronounced Reece-ling) which is consumed in vast quantities in this country. The wine produced is similar in style to, but slightly sweeter than, Liebfraumilch, and is made in the area of Lutomer.

Yugoslavia's red wines are not seen very often in this country and are generally very hot, alcoholic wines. Recent plantings of Cabernet Sauvignon have, however, produced some decent wines.

Bulgaria

Bulgaria, a country which has been producing wine for centuries, has taken notice of wine drinking trends in Europe and has adapted its wines to follow

consumer demand. Excellent 'varietal' wines are found in Bulgaria, made from Cabernet Sauvignon, Merlot and Chardonnay. Whilst not up to the standard of many French equivalents, these are sound wines which represent excellent value for money for everyday drinking.

The Rest of the World

Over the last ten years the choice of wines available has increased dramatically. In Britain you can buy wines from virtually all the wine producing countries, from China to the United States.

The most important countries are those known as "New World" countries, including Australia, the United States, New Zealand and South Africa.

California

California's wines have become popular through sales of carafe wine – offering the added bonus of re-using the carafe after you have drunk the wine.

However, there is more to California than re-usable carafes. Wine production in California is enormous, and huge amounts of 'jug' wines are drunk there. They often come from one of California's hottest regions, the San Joaquin Valley, and are similar in quality to French table wines.

The Californians are fortunate that their climate is so well suited to viticulture, although the climate does vary enormously across the state.

There is rarely a shortage of sunshine, in fact the weather is so consistently good that an 'off' vintage (as found in Europe) is virtually unheard of. However, this does create problems with water shortages. Fortunately, the Californian wine producers are allowed to irrigate their vineyards, whereas in most European wine producing areas irrigation is forbidden.

Many Californian wines are big, beefy, powerful wines, normally high in alcohol. They are not the kind of wines to drink at lunchtime if you intend doing any work in the afternoon. The best can rival Europe's top wines and, although their wines have always been rather larger than life, the more innovative producers are now trying to produce more elegant, European-style wines with more finesse.

The best Californian wines come from the Napa Valley and Sonoma County. If the

Though without the centuries of tradition of the European wineries, the vineyards of California (facing page) produce some excellent wines.

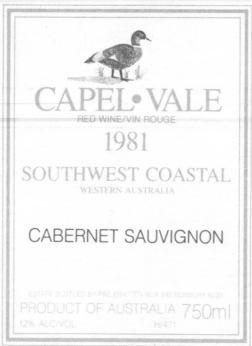

wine is of a good quality, the area as well as the individual estate and/or the name of the winery will be indicated on the label. Small wineries, which generally produce the top quality wines, are known as *boutique* wineries.

Californian wines are classed as *varietals*, a term which simply means they are mainly made from one grape variety. Amongst the red grapes grown are several of Bordeaux's leading varieties; particularly successful is the red Cabernet Sauvignon. Unlike wines from Bordeaux, where the varieties are blended, the Californians like to keep theirs pure.

Red Californian Wines
Zinfandel is California's most widely planted red grape, and produces a wine people either love or hate because of its highly individual flavour.

It can produce very full, heavy wines, often as high as 13% to 14% alcohol – an ordinary French table wine would be about 11% alcohol. They also make port-style wines from this grape. In contrast, it also produces lighter, Beaujolais-style wines.

Other red grape varieties are Merlot and some Pinot Noir.

White California Wines
The most widely planted white grape is Tompson's Seedless. However, this is not seen much on labels as it is mainly used for jug wines and for blending, and makes rather bland wines.

The Chardonnay grape of white burgundy fame produces deliciously rich, full, dry white wines, normally higher in alcohol and heavier than their European counterparts.

Other varieties to look out for on labels are Fumé Blanc (the Sauvignon of the Loire), Johannisberg or Rhine Riesling, Colombard, Chenin Blanc and Gewürztraminer.

Several other states in America produce wine; among the most important are New York State, Washington and Oregon.

Chile
Chile is probably the most interesting of the South American countries producing wine. Mainly made in large co-operatives, Chilean wines, particularly the reds, are

good value for money. The reds are quite full, spicy wines with lots of flavour but without excesses of tannin (a bitter substance which comes from the grape skins). Cabernet Sauvignon is the most important red grape, followed by Merlot and Malbec. The white wines are generally not so interesting, often lacking the acidity to make them properly balanced.

Red Chilean bag-in-box wines are worth buying – the wine seems to have the ability to survive this type of packaging far more successfully than most of its European counterparts.

Chile has the potential to produce some very fine wines. Meanwhile, take advantage of the sound, good value reds already available in this country.

Australia

Australia has been shipping wine to England since the 1800s. Australians

Facing page: the contrast in style of Australian wine labels emphasises the many types of wine produced in that country. Around the town of Griffith in New South Wales is a vast area of irrigated land (this page), known as the Murrumbidgee, which produces a fair amount of Australia's wine.

Top: huge wooden presses with their solid columns and massive screws, in a German cellar. Bottom: grape juice lies in large wooden vats in a French winery, before being transferred to fermenting vessels.

themselves consume a large quantity of their wine, and there are a respectable number of serious producers, some of whose wineries have been producing wine for over a century. Many of the best wines are only made in very small quantities in *boutique* wineries, and examples of these now reach Britain. Probably the most important of these is Petaluma, whose wines are well worth searching out.

In the past, Australia produced quantities of fortified wine, often rather heavy and alcoholic, but lacking charm. Since then wine-making techniques have improved immeasurably, and excellent everyday table wines are now being made and have overtaken production of fortifed wines. Many of the best bag-in-box wines are Australian, which is not surprising since they pioneered the technique. Unlike most European bag-in-box producers, the Australians put good quality wines rather than the cheapest table wines in their boxes.

Australia's wines are divided into states and regions, of which the Hunter

River Valley, to the north of Sydney, is one of the best. Here the most widely planted red grape is the Shiraz, related to the Syrah grown in the Rhône, and the Semillon, known rather confusingly as the Hunter Riesling. Coonawara, in South Australia, bordering Victoria, produces big, rich red wines from the Shiraz and Cabernet Sauvignon grapes. Surprisingly, despite the flat, dusty plains, the region is now producing top quality wines made from the Riesling grape.

Across the board, Australian wine-makers are amongst the best in the world. They grow and vinify a wide variety of grapes ranging from the German Riesling to the French Chenin Blanc. Few countries can compete with such a diverse range of grapes and fine wines.

New Zealand

Wines from New Zealand really started to become popular during the Second World War when, to keep up with the thirst of incoming American servicemen, more wine had to be produced.

New Zealand, although often classed along with Australia (it's over 1,000 miles away!) and California in wine terms, is very different because of its relatively temperate climate. As a result, the New Zealanders planted Müller-Thurgau to make dry and medium-dry white wines, light in style, and the light, spicy Gewüztraminer.

South Africa

Although it's only relatively recently that we have started to see South African wines in this country they have been produced for over 300 years. In the 18th century, for example, South Africa produced a famous sweet wine called Constantia.

In 1973, South Africa's Wine of Origin legislation was passed and the vineyards were divided into fourteen main areas. All the wines have to pass strict controls and only the very best are allowed the word *Superior* on their quality seal. South African labels have a series of coloured seals on them: the blue stripe states the region of origin, the red the vintage year and the green the grape variety used. Wines can only carry the word *Estate* if they are bottled at the vineyard from which they are produced.

In general, the best wines are produced near to the coast and are less 'cooked' than those made inland. Many of the country's finest wines are fortified dessert wines and sherries, although single varietal wines are getting better and better. Grapes most frequently used include Cabernet Sauvignon, Cabernet Franc, Shiraz and Pinotage for the reds, and, for the whites, Chenin Blanc (also known as Steen), Kerner and Riesling. The Chenin Blanc, when grown in South Africa, produces a much crisper and drier wine than the wines of the Loire Valley. Many South African white wines are slightly pétillant (fizzy), which helps keep them on the light side, while the red wines are characteristically round and soft and, although far from sweet, have an underlying rich, ripe fruit flavour.

Below: the ordered verdancy of the vineyards around the South African university town of Stellenbosch.

Much of South Africa's wine is made by large groups, KWV, Stellenbosch Farmers' Winery and The Bergkelder (who make the Fleur de Cap range), all of whom produce wine of respectable quality. Although South Africa is not as advanced as California or Australia, she is beginning to produce good quality wines.

Exclusive Meals for Fine Wine

The recipes on the following pages have all been selected for the way in which they complement fine wine. The ingredients and the suggested wine (and it is only a suggestion) may be expensive, but I think you will find the end result to be something rather special.

Faisan aux Marrons

Remove the legs from two pheasants. Skin the breasts, detach them from the carcase and season with salt and pepper. Place in a heavy saucepan and let them cook slowly with a knob of butter for about 8 minutes on each side. Remove from the pan and add a wineglass of sherry and one of cognac. Add ½ pint veal stock with 2 ounces of foie gras or foie gras purée diced small. Let the sauce reduce by half. Add 4 soup spoons of double cream and 2 ounces of butter mixing well. Pipe round the edge of the dish a purée of chestnuts, you may also place around the breasts some whole peeled and cooked chestnuts. Arrange the breasts on the dish and pour the sauce over.

You could use the legs, but naturally they will take longer to cook.

Corton-Grancey 1969
or Corton-Grancey 1973

Château Beychevelle is one of the anomalies of the claret business. Officially classified in 1855 as a 4th Growth, it is rated by most of those who know to be well worth the company of 2nd Growths.

It is a wine of character, one of the best St Juliens I know. Its name has a curious origin — if the story is to be believed. The property was at one time owned by the Duc d'Eperon, Grand Admiral of France. It overlooks the estuary of the Gironde, and ships sailing past the Château were ordered "baissez les voiles" (strike sail). Hence the corruption to Beychevelle. Well, it's a nice story . . .

Carré d'Agneau en Croûte

This really is a delicacy and so well worth doing. It can all be prepared two or three days in advance and kept in the refrigerator for cooking when required.

Skin and bone some best end of lamb. Cut away the fat so that only a thin layer remains and keep the fat as intact as possible. Spread the veal stuffing. Then fold the fat over the whole joint spread with the veal mixture and tie it up. Cook for three minutes on each side, in a heavy pan and on maximum heat on top of the cooker. Never give more than 6 minutes in total and do not even try to roast this dish in the oven. Remove the meat and leave it on one side to cool. Roll out puff pastry and envelop the carré completely. It looks best if you can trace fancy designs on the pastry, like hearts or diamonds. Glaze the pastry and bake for anything from 25 to 45 minutes according to whether or not you like pink lamb. Serve with madeira or perigourdine sauce. (Allow 1 best end of lamb for 2 persons).

For the stuffing, mince $\frac{1}{2}$ pound of veal and mix with purée of mushroom, tarragon, seasoning, a dessert spoon or two of brandy and about $\frac{1}{2}$ cup of double cream, to a stiff consistency.

Chevalier-Montrachet

Imagine a relatively small sports stadium: a football pitch or a baseball diamond, plus a few extras like a tennis court or two and a pitch-and-putt fun course. Tilt it sharply, so that walking up it becomes an effort as strenuous as playing ball would be on the level. Cover the surface with stones, expose it to hail in early spring and hot sun in August, and then you have a simulacrum of the Burgundian vineyard of *Chevalier-Montrachet*.

In a very good year this 18-acre vineyard produces not much more than 1,000 cases; and in a very good year this white wine is so superbly dry, so magnificently reminiscent of the stony soil from which it has perversely come that one feels privileged to taste it.

Grouse à la Crème Aigre

Take a grouse and put it in a hot pan with a stick of chopped celery and a sprig of thyme, and cook on each side for 9 minutes in a hot oven. Take out of the saucepan, cut off the breast and legs and keep warm. Chop the bones and put them in a saucepan with 2 tablespoons of vinegar and a glass of dry white wine. Add ⅓ pint of double cream, salt and pepper and let reduce until it has thickened. You may add sliced button mushrooms after you have strained the sauce. Serve with a purée of celery.

Ch. Lynch-Bages 1969

Château Lynch-Bages is another of those excellent wines of Pauillac which most people feel ought to be a classified 2nd Growth rather than its official 5th Growth. Certainly the market would seem to uphold this view, for Lynch-Bages costs more than many 3rd or 4th Growths.

It is a rounded wine, perhaps with a tendency to fade a little with advancing years, a tendency not at all noticeable in the 1969 vintage.

Perdreaux aux Olives

Roast a young partridge with about 4 ounces of small stoned green olives in a heavy pan, turning it after 10 minutes and basting. The partridge should take 20 minutes to cook. Take the partridge out of the pan and keep it warm. Put in the pan 3 ounces of finely minced green olives, ½ wine glass of dry white wine and ½ glass of veal stock. Let it reduce for about 10 minutes on a fast fire. Add about 2 ounces of butter and pour the sauce over the partridge.

Corton-Grancey 1969
Louis Latour

Any wine with the name Corton as part of its label is worthy of respect, for here you have the finest wines of Beaune, firm and fruity. *Corton-Grancey* is a fine specimen. It is not, in fact, the name of a vineyard, that second half of the title, but the name of the château in Aloxe-Corton where it is bottled by a first-class merchant and vineyard owner, Louis Latour.

Sauté de Veau Provençale

Use trimmings of veal from a leg that is to be roasted, or cut an escalope in strips, which will cost a little more. The strips should be about ¼-inch thick by a ½-inch wide. To each portion add two large or three medium tomatoes skinned and chopped (even pipped but that is not essential), one onion and half a clove of pressed garlic. Sauté the veal on a hot stove with hot butter and a bayleaf, stirring all the time but never allowing the butter to burn. It will need 5 minutes at the very most and would become tough if it ever boils or is overcooked.

Remove the veal and add to the chopped tomato-and-onion mixture a tablespoon of vinegar, some white wine and a few stoned, green olives. Two or three anchovy fillets are very good but for those who dislike anchovies they can be left out. Add a little meat stock, season, and put the veal strips back on the mixture. Serve with chopped parsley and some of the curly leaves to decorate. This tastes and looks very well on rice.

Moulin à Vent 1973
Groffier-Léger

The presence or absence of anchovy in the Mirabelle Sauté de Veau Provençale is crucial in determining which wine one should offer one's guests: indeed, this apparently small ingredient is almost a touchstone for the host who wishes to present just the right wine for the right dish at the right moment.

So, with anchovy, I recommend one of the great white wines of Burgundy. There are other wines which include the vineyard name Montrachet on their labels, and there will always be argument about which is supreme. Let the disputants dispute: suffice it for our purposes to say that the pale gold of *Puligny-Montrachet*, with its extraordinary scent coming up to one as the glass is swirled, represents a very good wine indeed, something for which we should be prepared to give silent thanks to whichever gods there may be.

What a difference a taste makes! For Sauté de Veau without anchovy I suggest another Beaujolais: this time, to blend with the subtlety of the sauce, I commend *Moulin à Vent 1973*.

Râble de Lièvre St Honorat

Take a saddle of hare. Remove the skin and put it in a dish with 1 stick of chopped celery, 1 onion, 1 chopped carrot, a sprig of thyme, a bay leaf and 1 glass of white wine and let it marinate for 24 hours.

Take it out of marinade, put it in a hot saucepan and cook for 5 minutes on each side. Take it out of the saucepan and keep it warm. Add the marinade to the saucepan with one soupspoon of redcurrant jelly, $\frac{1}{2}$ teaspoon of crushed peppercorn and $\frac{1}{2}$ pint stock. Let it reduce to two thirds, strain, and mix in 2 ounces of butter, $\frac{1}{2}$ pint of double cream, 3 ounces of sliced mushrooms and 3 soupspoons of vinegar. Stir until thick.

Châteauneuf du Pape
1972

Châteauneuf-du-Pape is one of the best-known wines from the whole of France. Why this should be so is difficult to know: perhaps it is because it is such a big-hearted wine, full and generous and good-tempered. It has a deep crimson colour, and is one of the stronger wines of the Rhone, up to 14% alcohol. It is made from a blend of around a dozen different grape varieties, though how vines at all can grow among the rocks of the high tableland devoted to vineyards is one of the small miracles of viticulture.

The "new castle" from which the wine takes its name is now a ruin: it was once the summer palace of the Popes of Avignon during the 14th century schism — Avignon and its pont is about 12 miles south, and the wine we now know as Châteauneuf-du-Pape was earlier simply known as Vin d'Avignon. By whatever name this is a most drinkable wine, especially with a strong meat dish such as Râble de Lièvre St Honorat.

Soufflé Roquefort

This is another of those dishes which leaves everybody guessing — once you have tried this you will scorn a plain cheese soufflé.

For liberal helpings for four people you need ½ pint of milk, 1 ounce of butter, 4 whole eggs, 1 heaped dessertspoon of plain flour and 4 ounces of Roquefort cheese. Have a greased mould ready and beat the egg yolks well, cover them and put aside. Melt the butter and add the flour, stirring to keep it smooth. Add the boiling milk while still stirring. To this roux add the beaten egg yolks, continuing to stir, then the Roquefort, seasoning and a dash of cayenne pepper. Set away from the stove to cool, while whipping the egg whites quickly to stiffen. Fold the whites into the cheese roux and pour all into the mould, making sure to leave about ½ inch from the top otherwise the soufflé will overflow and spoil. Bake for 15-20 minutes at 220 degrees Centigrade. Ambrosial with a glass of port.

Croft
Vintage 1963

As with champagne, so with vintage port. People settle on their favourites, and will be tempted away to no other, however distinguished the name. So the Taylor man will barely tolerate a Sandeman or a Cockburn, and he who has been weaned on Fonseca will scarcely nod in the direction of Warre or Dow.

Nonetheless, for the Soufflé Roquefort, I bravely commend a *Croft 1963*. It was John Croft who, in 1788, declared: 'An Englishman of a certain standing cannot do without a glass of port after a good dinner'. So let it be.

Coquilles St Jacques

Choose fresh scallops by the brightness and deep colour of the red parts. If that is dull they are not fresh enough. Some of the more exclusive frozen food firms sell good frozen scallops, although eaten beside the fresh ones, you will notice the difference.

Allowing four scallops per portion, this recipe will be sufficient for three persons. Put the scallops in a pan with three ounces of shrimps, 3 ounces of sliced mushrooms, a knob of butter, salt and pepper to taste and just cover with half dry white wine and half fish stock. Bring to the boil then let it simmer for about 6 minutes. Strain the stock; let it reduce to about two thirds. Add ½ pint of double cream and let it thicken. Put the scallops back in the sauce and pipe mashed potato around the edge of the shell. Place the scallops in the shells, keeping a drop of the sauce back. Add to the sauce ⅓ pint of double cream whipped with 2 egg yolks. Pour over the scallops, sprinkle some grated cheese on top and put under the grill to colour.

Pouilly Fumé de
Ladoucette 1973

A combination of the Sauvignon Blanc grape and the climate along the Loire near Nevers in the centre of France produces *Pouilly Fumé*, a pale white wine that has much more character than its colour might suggest. It accompanies most shellfish dishes perfectly.

Filets de Sole Marseillaise

Drees serves about 3 fillets per person, but 2 might well satisfy most people. Poach the fillets of sole in white wine and fish stock which just covers the fish and to which a pinch or two of the expensive shredded, not powdered, saffron has been added. In a maximum of 10 minutes, according to the size of the fillets, rest the sole on a pre-cooked pilaff of rice which should have been strained in cold water to separate grains if there is the slightest sign of stickiness when the rice has cooked. Put the dish with rice and fillets into a warm oven. Quickly make a sauce with reduced stock, double cream, seasoning and a tiny knob of butter. The sauce should look pale golden yellow. Strain the sauce over the dish and

serve. *This looks very good garnished with little pink pieces of lobster or salmon, with prawns or with baby button mushrooms. Once covered with sauce, it can keep for a very short while as your guests finish their pre-dinner drink but do not let it overcook and do not let the sauce solidify, so time it well.*

Gewurtztraminer — Hugel

Gewurtztraminer is a grape that produces a slightly spicy wine which is instantly recognisable both to palate and to nose. Certainly, the best of its product comes from Alsace in those distinctive slender green flutes, and the House of Hugel is rightly proud of this example.

Croustade de Saumon

Now here is a way of using salmon tails. I happen to love the tail, not only because it is always cheaper but because I like its firmness.

Put the boned fish into a pan with some melted butter and seasoning. Cook it gently for 5 to 6 minutes per side (rather less for leftover, cooked fish). Add chopped, cooked leaf spinach or cooked sorrel, double cream

and more seasoning if needed. Lay the spinach or sorrel in the middle of some rolled, flat puff pastry and, on top, spread the salmon. Sprinkle with a little nutmeg and add a knob of butter. Fold the pastry edges to cover the filling. Glaze the top with milk or beaten egg yolk and then bake for 25 minutes or until nicely brown. Serve with melted butter mixed with a drop of lemon juice. Never make in advance and rewarm — prepare the raw materials and serve as soon as it is baked.

Sparkling Vin Fou
Brut Renaissance —
Henri Maire

No fashionable wine comes from the Jura, which is a pity, because the vineyards along the foothills of the mountain range yield wines which are always interesting, if some way from the first-class.

    Vin Fou is, really, a fun wine: easy on the palate and something to talk about other than the excellence of the

Apples or Pears in Wine

Choose a William Pear or a Cox's Orange Pippin apple. Peel the fruit and add white wine to some syrup of Grand Marnier. Poach the fruit in a close-fitting dish for 15 minutes with the wine syrup halfway up the sides. Then cook for a further 7-8 minutes, ladling wine over the fruit but do not let the fruit break and fall apart.

    You will need very little syrup as the fruits are sweet and should be ever so slightly acid when served. You can keep any unused wine in the fridge and use over and over again with fruit.

Strawberry Gâteau

You will need 4 eggs, 4 ounces of caster sugar and 4 ounces of plain flour. Never have self-raising flour in the kitchen if you want to acquire the Robinson touch. It robs you of complete control — even plain flours vary but nothing like to the same degree of their self-raising counterparts. Whip the eggs and sugar in a bowl standing in a double pan until the mixture makes a strong thread from the end of the whisk, then fold in the flour and transfer immediately to pre-greased moulds, preferably of the type with a base that slides out. When cooked — which will take about 10-15 minutes at 220 degrees Centigrade, allow to cool slightly.

Turn out on to a wire tray and slice in half when cold. Prepare in advance a little syrup made from sugar and water and add Kirsch in the proportion of one part Kirsch to two parts syrup. Pour into a bottle with a sprinkler cork, or a cork with a 'V'-shaped cut, and shake the Kirsch syrup all over the sponge to moisten it whilst keeping it firm and whole. Spread a thick layer of cream over the bottom half and arrange large strawberries that have been halved to cover the cream. Cover the strawberries with a further thin layer of whipped cream, then add the top half of the sponge. Add a further layer of cream then more strawberries, leaving a rim of half an inch around the edge.

The gâteau can be made with other fruits. With raspberries, it is delicious. It is equally excellent with apricots and sliced peaches but these are apt to look pale and need the addition of some fresh or glacé cherries for colour.

This can be made in advance for an evening dinner party and will keep firmly in the refrigerator all day. Do remember, however, to take it out at least 40 minutes before serving if you want its full taste.

Champagne G.H. Mumm
Cordon Rouge NV

Like several of the other great champagne houses of Reims, Epernay and Ay that grew up on the banks of the Marne, the House of G. H. Mumm was founded by a German. The first Herr Mumm came from a distinguished family of wine-makers at Rudesheim on the Rhine, and

started making champagne in Reims in 1827. His grandson, G. H. Mumm himself, joined the firm in 1838, and gave it his initials in 1853, and the firm continued to be family-owned and family-run up to the outbreak of the First World War. Alas, no Mumm had thought to take out French citizenship. The family were treated as enemy aliens, their property sequestered; the firm put up for public auction in 1920. Through it all, somehow, the champagne maintained its high quality.

Mumm's Cordon Rouge is now one of the largest of the grande marque champagne houses, and its famous red stripe, and the designation Cordon Rouge, on its bottles have undoubtedly helped to make it recognisable on both sides of the Atlantic.

Peach Robert

Buy a tin of whole white peaches; the best are from Japan. Stone them without damaging, and fill the hole with marinated glacé fruits, crumbled praline, or experiment yourself with a suitable filling. Line a dish with a sponge base or with sponge fingers. Lay the peaches in the dish and then whip the cream with a little Kirsch or other favourite liquor until it is slightly stiff, because it must be soft enough to pour over the peaches and the sponge. A variation is to tint the cream slightly pink and add a glacé cherry atop each peach.

Champagne has its devotees more than any other type of wine, and it is surprising how devoted they are to their favourite marque. Here is one man who swears by Bollinger; another who calls for a bottle of The Widow (Veuve Cliquot) and will have no alternative; Laurent Perrier has its following, as has Moet & Chandon, Mercier and the others in a grand litany of pleasure.

Crêpes Farcies

These are pancakes filled with a soufflé mixture (without egg whites), flavoured with any liqueur, for example Grand Marnier, Cointreau or Drambuie to name my favourites. Warm the mixture and add the liqueur. Fill the pancakes and place on a buttered dish in the oven for 5 to 6 minutes, at 218 degrees Centigrade.

An excellent alternative is apple, although many fillings can be used. Peel, core and chop 2 or 3 large Bramley cooking apples. Melt 1 ounce of butter in a pan, tip in the apples and stir in 3 ounces of caster sugar. Cook on a high gas to keep the apples white, stirring all the time with a wooden spoon. Take them from the heat before they become purée, and place in a strainer to drain away the surplus juice. Place a tablespoonful of apple in each pancake and fold over. Arrange on the dish and return to the oven for 5 minutes.

Ch. Climens 1970

Everybody knows Château d'Yquem, that king of sweet white wine from Sauternes. Not so many know its nearest rival from Barsac. *Château Climens*, like Yquem in many ways, is unlike it in that it is better comparatively young. The 1970 is just right: the wine is light, with a subtle sweetness that never cloys: a fantastic dessert wine, which has made a wonderful recovery from frost devastation in 1956.

The cocktails illustrated here are based on various wines, including sherry, vermouth and Dubonnet. The Sherry Cobbler (far left) is made by filling a glass with crushed ice and adding sherry, orange curaçao and sugar syrup. The Americano (second from left) is a mixture of sweet vermouth and Campari topped up with soda water. Kir (third from left) is made by pouring a teaspoonful of crème de cassis into a goblet and topping up with chilled white wine. To make a Champagne Cocktail (third from right), seen here served in a sugar-frosted glass, soak a lump of sugar in Angostura bitters, add a little brandy and fill the glass with ice-cold champagne. The Spritzer (second from right) is a perfect summer drink – dry white wine and soda water; and Dubonnet, cherry brandy, orange juice, lemon juice and egg white are shaken, strained and topped up with soda water to produce a Dubonnet Fizz (far right).

Wine Cocktails

'From wine what sudden friendship springs!'
John Gay.

Broadly defined as 'the fermented juice of grapes',
the term wine is used to cover sherry, port,
vermouth and other wine-based aperitifs, madeira,
champagne, sparkling wine and, of course, wine
itself. Both port and sherry are wines fortified with
brandy, port coming from the Douro valley in
Portugal, and sherry, originally, from the province
of Cadiz in Spain. Vermouth, whose name derives
from 'wermut,' the German word for wormwood, is
usually based on white wine (the red being
coloured with caramel), and flavoured with
aromatic ingredients including herbs,
spices, roots and fruit peels.

ADONIS

Stir two parts dry sherry with one part sweet vermouth and a dash of orange bitters. Add a twist of orange peel.

ALFONSO

Dissolve a lump of sugar in a couple of dashes of Angostura bitters at the bottom

Below: Bamboo. Facing page: Black Magic.

of the glass, add a measure of Dubonnet and top up with chilled champagne. Stir gently and add a twist of lemon peel.

AMERICANO

Over ice cubes pour one part sweet vermouth and one part Campari. Top up with soda water and garnish with a slice of orange or a twist of lemon peel.

BAMBOO

Stir one part dry sherry with one part dry vermouth and a dash of orange bitters. Add a twist of lemon peel.

BELLINI

Pour a little peach juice into the glass and top up with chilled champagne.

BLACK MAGIC

Squeeze the juice of two grapes into the glass, add two dashes of Mandarine Napoléon and top with dry, sparkling wine. Drop one black grape into the drink and put another on the rim of the glass.

BLACK VELVET

Into a glass pour equal parts chilled champagne and Guinness.

BRAZIL

Stir one part dry sherry with one part dry vermouth, a dash of Angostura bitters and a dash of pastis. Add a twist of lemon peel.

BUCK'S FIZZ

Pour freshly squeezed orange juice into a glass and add champagne in a ratio of one part orange juice to two parts champagne.

CARDINALE

Pour a little crème de cassis into a glass and top up with dry, red wine.

CHAMPAGNE COCKTAIL

Drop a lump of sugar into the glass and soak it with Angostura bitters. Add a couple of dashes of brandy and top with chilled champagne. Garnish with a slice of orange and a cherry.

DUBONNET FIZZ

Shake together three parts Dubonnet, one part cherry brandy, two parts fresh orange juice, two parts fresh lemon juice and an egg white. Top up with soda water.

FINO MAC

Stir two parts dry sherry with one part ginger wine.

FRAISE ROYALE

Blend two fresh strawberries with a dash of